Dog Life

Celebrating the History, Culture & Love of the Dog

D1500468

AMY SHOJAI

FURRY MUSE PUBLICATIONS

FURRY MUSE
PUBLICATIONS
P.O. Box 1904, Sherman, TX 75091
www.SHOJAI.com

Illustrations and Photos on designated pages credited below are Licensed via DepositPhotos.com unless otherwise noted:
Front Cover ©kisscsanad (Golden), Back Cover ©vikarus (Border Collie)

2: ©fotymam, spaniel at gate
3: ©skavapolo via yayimages.com, Hohenzollern Castle (Germany) coat of arms
5: ©lifeonwhite, white dog play-bowing
6: ©vikarus, dog with horse
8: ©averyanova, dogs playing in water
10: ©mrdoomits, dog and fence
12: ©ruskpp, miacids; © PhotosVac, grey wolf; © CoreyFord, Dire wolf; Hespercyon via commons.wikimedia.org
13: Amphicyon via commons.wikimedia.org
14: ©PhotosVac, Thylacine
16: ©ekays, dingo
17: ©mikelane45, Cape Hunting Dog; ©assoonas, Dhole
18: ©tiger_barb, group of dingoes
19: ©Nazzu, Bush Dog; ©Voren1, Raccoon Dog
10: ©zaitsevainna, Artic Fox; ©Drago_Nika, Red Fox
21: ©EastmanPhoto, Fennec; ©fouroaks, jackals fighting
22: ©belizar, Mained Wolf; ©pictureguy, via yayimages, Coyote
23: ©Alexandra Lande, Asiatic Wolf
24: ©JimCumming, wolves
25: ©dlpn, Anubis
27: ©outsiderzone, golden Anubis; ©dlpn, clay Dingo
28: ©mj0007, dog vase
29: ©markomolan1, Anubis
30: ©Malgorzata_kistryn, dog gargoyle
31: ©georgios, hare hunting; ©marzolino, Greyhounds
32: ©dlpn, Chinese golden dogs
34: ©marzolino, French dogs
35: ©Marinaplevako, Afghan
37: ©hzparisien@gmail.com, knight and dog
38: ©Farinosa, French Bulldog
40: ©izanbar, mosaic
41: ©spaxiax, Chekov
42: ©eriklaur, Newfoundland
43: ©lifeonwhite, Collie
44: ©videokvadrat, Samoyed
45-49: PD-art, via commons.wikimedia.org
47: ©catalby, dog bites dragon
59: ©joymsk, hunter with dogs; ©galdzer, Diana; ©elesi, St. Martire
51: ©PD-art, illuminated folio; ©Reinhardhauke, stained glass, via commons.wikimedia.org
52: ©Izumifuchu, coat of arms
52-53: ©lifeonwhite, Dachshunds
54: ©zatletic, Hercules & Cerberus
55: ©amuzica, dog face
57: ©Drago_Nika, Weimaraner
59-60: PD, via commons.wikimedia.org

61: ©Brusnikaphoto, Saluki
62-63: ©cynoclub, 5 terriers
65: ©Mike Peele (mikepeel.net) via commons.wikimedia.org
66: ©bilisanas, German Shepherd
67: ©artlosk, Kyrgyzstan monument
68: ©nstanev, Patton; ©tdoes1, FDR; ©lifeonwhite, Bull Terrier
69: ©noskaphoto, SAR
70: ©XiXinXing, guide dog
71: ©VolodymyrBur, Golden on beach
72: ©megastocker, Anubis
73: ©Fotoskat, fashion dog via yayimages.com
74: ©FotoJagodka, Rottweiler
75: ©AlexanderPokusay, dog bones
76: ©Biganolt, Puli
77: ©FotoJagodka, Shih Tzu
78: ©lifeonwhite, dog eating
79: ©marinini, eyes
80: ©FotoJagodka, French Bulldog
81: ©Willeecole, Pointer pup
82: ©graphicphoto, dog on back
83: ©feedough, dog bark
85: ©firstbite, jumping up; ©DepsitNovic, digging
86: ©graphicphoto, barking
87: ©Gordo25, nursing pups
90-91, ©lifeonwhite, Dalmatians
92: ©daniaalexa, Yorkie
93: ©photodesign, Frisbee dog
94: ©lunamarina, chewing dog
95: ©cynoclub, Malinois
96: ©Fotosmurf, 2 pups, via yayimages.com
97: ©aetb, old dog, via yayimages.com
98: ©derepente, Basenji
100: PD, via commons.wikimedia.org
101: ©mdorothya, carrier
102-103: ©Carlosobriganti, dog at sunset
104: ©averyanova, hose dog
105: ©pajche, dog in water
108: ©belchonok, pup exam
109: ©goga18128.mail.ru, Greyfriars Bobby; ©cowardlion, Hachiko
111: ©cynoclub, old dog, via yayimages.com
112: ©Carmelka, Borzoi
114: ©Mayalain, agility
116: ©herreid, Australia Terrier
117: ©Studiotrapeza, Bouvier
118-119: ©willeecole, Bulldogs
120: ©CaptureLight, Chessie
120-121: ©Foto-front, Shar-Pei

122: ©averyanova, Chow
123: ©glenkar, Irish Red & White Setter
124: ©dionoanomalie, Chin; ©CaptureLight, Water Spaniel; ©studiotrapeza, Komondor
125: ©imagebrokermicrostock, Kuvatz; ©toloubaev, Maltese; ©adogslifephoto, Labs
126: ©f8grapher, Lhasa Apso via yayimages.com; ©Madrabothair, Otter Hound
127: ©cynoclub, Rottweiler
128: ©ckellyphoto, Swissie
130: ©rook, Xolo via yayimages.com
131: ©f8grapher, Affen; ©lifeonwhite, Mal; ©vivienstocks, Akita; ©wacpan, Airedale
132: ©Farinosa, Basenji; ©lifeonwhite, Aussie, Staffie, Basset
133: ©FotoJagodka, Bedlington; ©Meldes, Beagle; ©lifeonwhite, Beardie, Berner
134: ©feedough, Bichon; ©adogslifephoto, Bloodhound; ©lifeonwhite, Border Collie; ©willeecole, Coonhound
135: ©eriklam, Border Terrier; ©FotoJagadka, Boxer; ©lifeonwhite, Boston, Briard
136: ©studiotrapeza, Brussels; ©lifeonwhite, Cairn; ©cynoclub, Brittany, Bullmastiff
137: ©lifeonwhite, Cav, Chihuahua, Clubmer, Chinese Crested.
138: ©willeecole, Dogue, ©lifeonwhite, Cocker, Dobie, Dandie
139: ©lifeonwhite, Greyhound, Irsh & Gordon Setter, Dane
140: ©lifeonwhite, Flat-Coated, Ger. Shorthaired Pointer; ©FotoJagodka, Finnish Spitz, GSD
141: ©lifeonwhite, JRT; ©cynoclub, Kerry Blue; ©vivienstocks, IG; ©FotoJagodka, Wolfhound
142: ©FotoJagodka, Mastiff; ©Cynoclub, Lakeland, Manchester, Min Pin.
143: ©FotoJagodka, Peke; ©Cynoclub, Papillon; ©lifeonwhite, Old English, Newfie
144: ©lifeonwhite, PBGV; ©FotoJagodka, Pom, Pharoah; ©cynoclub, Poodle
145: ©lifeonwhite, Pyrenees; ©cynoclub, Portie; ©FotoJagodka, Ridgeback, Pug
146: ©cynoclub, Staffie; ©lifeonwhite, St. Bernard; ©FotoJagodka, Tibbie; ©dionoanomalia, Wheaten
147: ©lifeonwhite, Schipperke; ©cynoclub, Scottie, Schnauzer, Shelties
148: ©cynoclub, Husky; ©FotoJagodka, Shiba; ©lifeonwhite, Shi Tzu, Skye
149: ©cynoclub, Tibetan Terrier; ©FotoJagodka, Welch Springer; ©Miraswonderland, Corgi
150: ©dionoanomalia, Westie: ©cynoclub, Griffon; ©Laures, Yorkie; ©lifeonwhite, Fox Terrier, Whippet

PUBLISHER'S NOTE: Every effort has been made to ensure that the information contained in this book is complete and accurate. However, neither the publisher nor the author is engaged in rendering professional advice or services to the individual reader. The ideas, procedures, and suggestions contained in this book are not intended as a substitute for consulting with your pet's physician.

Dog Life

Celebrating the History, Culture & Love of the Dog

DEDICATION

This book is dedicated to the dogs that never find
a home; in loving memory.

TABLE OF CONTENTS

	INTRODUCTION	9
ONE:	EVOLUTIONARY DOG	11
TWO:	CULTURED CANINE	39
THREE:	PHYSICAL DOG	73
FOUR:	GALLERY OF BREEDS	113
	ABOUT THE AUTHOR	151
	FURTHER READING	153
	INDEX	154

Introduction

No other animal has shared as much with humanity as *Canis familiaris*, the domestic dog. Indeed, for at least 32,000 years, this creature, but one paw-step away from the wolf, has willingly and happily traded freedom for an uncertain relationship with humankind.

Our relationship with the dog has spanned the gamut of our experience. The dog was a silent, uncelebrated partner at *Homo sapien's* own beginnings. Later targeted as an object of superstitious scorn, the dog was called "werewolf" or worse. Yet the dog's greatest role has been as partner and beloved companion.

Whether exploited, despised, or pampered, the dog has remained our staunchest companion. Dogs have hunted, gone to war, and been both beaten and rewarded by humans; they have retrieved our game and guarded our flocks; and they have loved us with unconditional fervor.

Why do humans love dogs? There are a variety of reasons—dogs are cute as puppies, and handsome as adults; they depend on us; pedigreed animals are a status symbol. But ultimately, we love dogs because they love us. Our dog loves us in spite of all our flaws and wriggles with delight at the mere sound of our step at the door.

The dog-and-human partnership is a symbiotic relationship that defies rational explanation. To a person, a dog may be a wild creature to be caressed and tamed, a mirror to reflect one's emotions, a sharer of sorrows, a giver of happiness, or a bringer of peace. I don't know why dogs love people; I'm just glad they do.

Dog Life is a book for dog lovers everywhere. It's a celebration of canine lore and history, and includes basic guidance for novice and seasoned dog fanciers alike. I hope these pages will touch the heart, lift the spirit, and broaden the reader's understanding of the nature of these marvelous creatures that have chosen to share their lives with us.

The dog can be a gift to the human soul. May we be worthy of such devotion.

One:
Evolutionary Dog

The pudgy puppy playing tug-of-war with your socks hasn't yet been in the house a full day, and already he's made himself a part of the family. He's left toothmarks on the La-Z-Boy recliner, pooped under the piano bench, and begged and wagged his way into your lap where he now snuggles with a happy little sigh. The longer the dog stays, the harder it will become to imagine life without him.

Dogs as we know them have been part of human lives for many thousands of years. Dogs buried with human remains dating 14,000 years ago were found in Germany, offering a strong case for domestication. More recently, dog skulls found in Siberia date from 36,000 B.P. and Belgium 33,000 B.P.

Even before humans began domesticating wild canids, dog ancestors shared human history. A fossil site at Zhoukoudian near Beijing, China, shows evidence that early *Homo erectus* and wolves lived in the same environment as early as 500,000 years ago. There is no proof that these wolves were domesticated, however.

Dogs are carnivorous (meat-eating)

"In the beginning, God created man, but seeing him so feeble, He gave him the dog."

Toussend

mammals, which are classified within the Order Carnivora and Family Canidae. Canids possess large, conical, canine teeth for puncturing and tearing flesh, and elongated bladelike "carnassial" cheek teeth for shearing meat. Modern land carnivores are all classified within the sub-order Fissipeda, which means "Cleft Foot" (having toes, as opposed to carnivores with fin-feet, like seals). Fissipeds appeared about 61 million years ago during the middle Paleocene epoch, and quickly diversified into new types of animals. Some became plant eaters, while others developed into even more accomplished land carnivores.

Miacids were small, shrewlike animals, the largest only about the size of a fox and the smallest about the size of a ferret. Their bodies were long, with relatively short legs, flat feet, and a long, extended tail. They probably looked like modern-day pine martins. Miacids were remarkably successful, forest-dwelling carnivores, and fossils showing skull size tell us that they were much smarter than their ancestors. Scientists speculate the Miacids had retractable claws and were arboreal (tree-climbing), much like today's house cats.

Grey Wolf

Dire Wolf

Hesperocyon

Miacid

This resemblance of a dog ancestor to cats isn't surprising. Carnivores include members of the bear family (Ursidae), the badger family (Mustelidae), the hyena family (Hyaenidae), the civet, genet, and mongoose family (Viverridae), the raccoon family (Procyonidae), the cat family (Felidae), and, of course, the entire dog, fox, and wolf family (Canidae).

Members of the family Miacidae were early carnivores that gave rise to all the modern families of the Order Carnivora at the beginning of the Oligocene epoch, about 40 million years ago. This means that dogs and cats are actually distantly related. Could this have something to do with the supposed ancient enmity between the two species?

Miacids are found at the base of the family tree; they branch into two distinct evolutionary paths: the Aeluroidea or "Catlike Form," and the Canoidea, the "Doglike Form." The Catlike forms (Viverridae, Hyaenidae, and Felidae) have retained the solitary stalk-and-pounce behavior of their Miacid ancestors.

The Canoids apparently originated as hunters in the open grasslands. The digitigrade (toe-walking) foot enabled these mammals to run faster over longer distances than many other carnivores. Claws became blunted, and paws were no longer used like hands to capture or manipulate prey (as in cats). Instead, canid jaws developed into the characteristically elongated snout, which is better adapted to capture and hold the prey.

Some species (like modern Cape Hunting Dogs and wolves) developed social "pack" hunting, a practice that enabled them to bring down much larger game. With communal hunting came a need for better communication, and sophisticated vocalizations, facial expressions and body scents, coded fur coloring for better distance identification, and the "semaphore" ear and tail-movement signals developed.

The flat-footed bear and the toe-walking dog diverged from the rest of the Canoidae in Oligocene times. Although they remain similar in general structure, bears became huge, almost totally herbivorous forest-dwelling animals, while the canids stayed smaller and remained more mobile carnivores.

Another Miocene species, *Amphicyon* ("Around Dog") was a gigantic, primarily herbivorous animal that was eventually replaced by the true bears. Today, many dog breeds still resemble, at least superficially, their Ursidae cousins.

Mesocyon, the "Half Dog," was a coyote-size animal that lived in the Miocene epoch, some 35 million years ago. The digitigrade foot and leg structure identified it as a forebear of the toe-walking, sprinting canines. Mesocyon was long-bodied and short-legged, with shearing carnassial teeth and a massive skull with a short muzzle. It probably looked more like a hyena than a dog.

Some early forms of canidae were exclusively carnivorous, as in the instance of *Hesperocyon,* which is the earliest recognized animal in the direct line of dog evolution. This dog was a small, house cat-size animal that hunted much like a modern fox, with stealth followed by a pounce.

The carnivore *Leptocyon* possessed a body and dentition that were recognizably foxlike in appearance. This animal appears in the fossil record in the late Oligocene and is in a direct ancestral line leading from the Miocene forms to the more modern *Canis.*

Scientists have never been able to prove with any certainty the direct wild ancestor of the dog. In the nineteenth century, Charles Darwin theorized that

Australia had a parallel evolution of dog-like marsupial creatures. The dog-headed pouched *Thylacine cynocephaus* also known as the Tasmanian Tiger or Tasmanian Wolf became extinct only 70 years ago.

crossbreeding the wolf, *Canis lupus*, and the golden jackal, *Canis aureus*, perhaps resulted in the forebears of today's dog. The theory held that certain dog breeds resembled the wolf, while others looked more like jackals.

Other scientists believed there was a separate unknown animal, now long extinct, from which our modern dogs evolved. However, no such "missing dog-link" has ever been found. More recently, both theories have been discredited.

Current theory postulates that modern domestic dogs are descended solely from wolves. Wolves evolved from a hyenalike animal, originating in the Western Hemisphere in the Oligocene epoch, and living through the Miocene epoch (about 15 million years ago). The wolf was probably domesticated during the Neolithic age, perhaps earlier. Fossilized bones of a small wolf (*Canis lupus variabilis*) have been found in a number of early-to-late Pleistocene locales in China along with *Homo erectus* remains, although there is no evidence that the wolf was domesticated at all. It is generally accepted that the basic ancestral animal was this or a similar subspecies of the wolf, and that China is one likely area of early domestication. Today, most experts agree that the wolf alone is the direct ancestor of our domestic dog.

Canine Cousins

The science of taxonomy, which classifies and defines links between different kinds of living things, is one of categories and divisions. Animals belong in the kingdom Animalia, in which they are further categorized into phylum, class, order, and family. Dogs are designated as the family Canidae. Animals grouped within the family are divided according to structural similarities; this category is known as the genus. Finally, animals within a genus are categorized by species, and some even further into subspecies. The species is the only taxonomic category that has biological meaning and may be tested through breeding experiments. Truly separate species cannot interbreed and produce fertile offspring. The subspecies, or variety, category is often evoked to name or describe hybrids.

About 10 million years ago, the family Canidae developed into the huge variety of animals that consists of the fourteen living genera we recognize today. Jackals, coyotes, wolves, and domestic dogs all share the same genus. All domestic dogs, no matter what their size or shape, belong to the family Canidae, genus *Canis*, species *familiaris*—our own "Familiar Dog."

WILD VERSUS TAME

The Cocker Spaniel puppy proudly carries a shoe into the family room, pauses, and sheepishly wags at your exclamation of surprise. As you try to retrieve the sneaker, you play a brief game of tug-of-war with the fiercely growling ball of fluff, before he relinquishes his prize, then yaps and bounces, begging for another game. Take a moment to consider: What exactly does that rambunctious, endearing puppy have in common with wild cousins in other parts of the world? How are they alike; what are their differences?

Canines all over the world are remarkably similar. Like all placental mammals, they have live births and suckle their young. Most canids have a gestation period of about sixty-three days, and their young are born with closed eyes and ears, and in large litters. Most canids are primarily meat eaters. The physical family likeness includes a long, typically doglike muzzle; large, mobile, erect ears; an expressive tail; and a muscular, agile body.

Most canids live in a small family group consisting of the male and female parents and first-year pups. Only wolves, the Dhole, and African Painted Dogs live in extended family communes. The hunting technique of these animals calls for speed and tirelessness, in which they simply wear down their prey in marathons of endurance, rather than using the stalk-and-ambush technique of cats.

The sheepdog tirelessly driving his flock reflects the mastery of the wolf that shadows the caribou and skillfully cuts out the weakest prey from the herd; the terrier ferrets out and catches rats with the dexterity of the fox; and the dog that raids the household garbage scavenges as naturally as the jackal.

Wild canids bark only when defending their den to draw attention and lead predators away. But their pups bark all the time, and so do most adult domestic dogs.

It's easy to see the many resemblances between the wild and the tame. Canids are physiologically so similar that all may potentially interbreed and produce fertile young. Dog- and-wolf crosses are not only possible but are quite common and often encouraged; offspring have characteristics of both parents. Dogs and jackals also can be easily crossed. There have even been hybrid animals produced from successful cross breeding of wolf, dog, and jackal.

Skeletal structure in wild canid species is very uniform, the most striking difference being size-related. This difference is primarily due to function. Obviously, in order for the northern wolf to capture the large prey of the tundra, it must be much bigger than the small Kit Fox, which subsists primarily on mice and rodents. Environment also dictates the distinctive fur coats among canids. The Arctic Fox wears white in winter to blend into the snowy background, then changes to slate gray to match the environment of warmer seasons.

Domestic dogs have been bred by humans into the wide range of shapes, colors, and sizes familiar to us today. This artificial selection of characteristics reflects the many purposes to which the domestic canine has been pressed. It hardly seems possible that the short legged, long-bodied Dachshund and the huge Neapolitan Mastiff could really belong to the same genus, let alone the same species.

Unfortunately, there is not space to discuss all of the many interesting varieties of the wild canids. Due to the great number, the following represents the most unusual or significant of the wild species.

Environment and food sources impact evolution and biodiversity even today. The "Sea Wolf" makes its home on the shorelines of Canada's Vancouver Island. Even the DNA of these German Shepherd-size island coastal wolves is different than the larger inland gray wolves. Also known as swimming wolves, they've been known to swim 7+ miles from island to rocky outcrops. About 90 percent of its diet is sea food.

Dingo

WILD DOGS

The term "wild dog" generally refers to a canid that hunts prey its own size or larger. All wild dogs rely on endurance to overcome their prey and are superb runners and trotters. Wild dogs have long, heavy jaws designed for crushing bones, and wide, short, bearlike ears located on the sides of their heads. Wild dogs live in packs or tribes made up of several generations. African Painted Dogs and Dholes are two examples of modern wild dogs.

African Painted Dog

Also known as the Cape Hunting Dog, the African Painted Dog is probably the most ancient of the wild dogs. Painted Dogs reach about 3.5 feet (1m) in length, have erect, bearlike ears, and live in the grasslands and open savannas south of the Sahara. Named *Lycaon pictus*, or "Painted Wolf," the African Painted Dog is the only wild canid to have irregular spotty markings of white, brown, and black. This unique coloration isn't camouflage, but instead serves as a means of visual identification over long distances.

The African Painted Dog is the only wild dog to have four toes on both fore and hind feet, rather than the typical five on the front and four on the back. It also has a functional collarbone, where most canids have only a remnant of cartilage.

The Painted Dog is a sight hunter, much like sighthound breeds of domestic dogs. It lives and hunts in large packs of up to sixty animals, roaming over wide areas to prey upon zebra, warthog, gazelle, and wildebeest. Families of Painted Dogs share their food by regurgitating partly digested meat to feed nursing females, the ill, and the young when the pack returns from hunting.

These canids are known for their comical and eager fascination with puppies. Upon return from a hunt, adults often stumble over each other in their eagerness to play with and feed the babies. Adults of both sexes often adopt orphaned pups to raise.

It is said that Assyrians and Egyptians used Painted Dogs from the fifth to the twelfth dynasty to course antelope. When replaced by a dog resembling the present-day Fox Terrier, Painted Dogs were abandoned and returned to the wild.

Dhole

The short-haired Dhole, *Cuon alpinus,* (Mountain Dog) is found on the Indian Subcontinent and in Southeast Asia. The Dhole resembles the fox, and typically has fox-red fur with a black-tipped tail. The Dhole communicates by whistles, cries, yaps, howls, barks, and whimpers. Primarily a forest dweller, the Dhole is a fearless, efficient hunter that will even attack tigers.

Beagles may be one of the most "talkative" of dog breeds. They were bred to bark as they hunt, and their joyous noise rivals any of the Dhole's communication.

Dingo

The Dingo, *Canis dingo,* is the only wild canid of Australia. This barkless dog reaches about 4 feet (1.2m) in length and is a silent hunter with strong jaws capable of breaking the spine of a kangaroo.

Some scientists believe Dingoes descended from the Phu Quoc dogs of eastern Asia or were carried to Australia by ancestors of the Aboriginal people. During the Pleistocene, when massive glaciers held much of the world's water frozen, lowered sea levels permitted early humans to cross the narrows between the Asiatic mainland and Australia. Australia was the Dingoes'

paradise. Within a few thousand years, Dingoes spread across Australia and displaced the marsupial "wolves" which are now extinct in all but a few remote areas of Tasmania.

The Basenji of North Africa not only looks very much like the Dingo, it is probably also descended from a similar canid ancestor. The Basenji is one of the oldest purebred dogs in existence and appears in Egyptian art that dates back 5,000 years. Like wild canids, adult Basenji dogs don't bark, unless taught by other domestic breeds.

Bush Dog

The Bush Dog, *Speothos venaticus,* looks like a squat, short-legged dog with a bear's head. All canids cock hindlegs and urinate to scent-mark territory, but female Bush Dogs back up and "handstand" to mark turf. The Bush Dog is a forest dweller that lives in dense undergrowth along rivers. It is an excellent swimmer and will go into the river after prey.

Several domestic breeds share the Bush Dog's fondness for water. In particular, retrievers like nothing better than swimming, and will dive enthusiastically into a pond, lake, river, or stream at the least provocation. While most boy dogs love to mark, we can be grateful they forego the handstand technique

Raccoon Dog

The Raccoon Dog, also called the Japanese Fox, *Nyctereutes procyonoides*, is found in China, Japan, and eastern reaches of Russia. Its thick, fleecy coat is colored and marked like that of the familiar raccoon. It lives in temperate and subtropical forests, along rivers or bushy areas, subsisting on a diet of fish, frogs, and acorns. The Raccoon Dog, unlike any other dog, is able to become semi-dormant during the winter months.

Terrier breeds were developed originally for eradicating vermin, and many continue to find great joy in hunting and catching rodents and other small game, just like the Raccoon Dog. As for hibernating, I personally know of several dogs that do a fair imitation.

The Artic Fox (left) becomes white to blend with the snow, while the Red Fox (below) has better cammouflage for woodlands.

Fox

"Fox" is the common name for all small wild canids, many outside the genus *Vulpes*. Foxes are smaller than wild dogs; none stand higher than the human knee, and many are as small as house cats. The fox hunts alone, and mainly at night, depending mostly on its senses of smell and hearing rather than on sight. In many ways, foxes are more like cats than dogs; they use cunning and stealth instead of speed in hunting. Moreover, the pupils of a fox's eyes close to slits just like those of a cat.

The fox's luxurious fur is highly prized by furriers the world over. As demand for its pelts grew, the fox became famous for its wiliness in evading hunters and trappers and was often celebrated for its cleverness and cunning in fable and folklore. The fox's weakness for blueberries, cherries, apples, grapes, sweet corn, squashes, and melons often tempt it to steal from field and vine.

In some cultures, it is believed that charms made in the likeness of the fox will bring success in business, because the fox's cunning affects the wearer.

The fox ranges from scorching deserts to the frozen Arctic. Some species, like the North American Gray Fox, *Urocyon cinereoargenteus*, prefer the woods and often climb trees to nest in hollows far above ground. The Fennec, *Fennecus zerda*, shown above, is strictly a desert animal that lives in excavations beneath sand dunes. Its enormous ears act both as radar and as radiators to help rid the body of excessive heat.

Jackal

Jackals, *Canis aureus,* are relatively small canids that reach a maximum body length of about 2.5 feet (75cm). Although jackals may prey on small animals, they mostly live off the leavings of others. Jackals are primarily nocturnal and rarely form packs; they usually live in pairs or in small families, much like the fox. Some bold jackals venture into villages and steal poultry, earning the enmity of humans. Do you know of a canine thief eager to swipe leavings from your dining table?

A god of ancient Egypt, Anubis conducted the souls of the dead, was the cleansing god, and the guardian of the gates of the underworld. Today, historians argue over whether Anubis was a jackal or the domestic dog. Both, it seems, had the same fondness for bodies of the dead.

Maned Wolf

The rare Maned Wolf, *Chrysocyon brachyurus*, may reach a body length in excess of 4 feet (1.2m), and is the largest South American canid. Its name comes from the luxuriant crest of long hair that extends from the nape of the neck to the shoulders. It has a distinctly foxy appearance, both in the shape of the face and fur coloring, but its long, narrow legs give the Maned Wolf a conspicuously odd look. The local people call it "fox-on-stilts," and indeed, it hunts by the fox's stalk-and-pounce method and buries excess food for its future use. Our dogs also cache leftover bones and sometimes toys for safekeeping.

Coyote

The Coyote, *Canis latrans*, looks like a small wolf. Coyotes were originally confined to the prairies of North America, where they preyed on prairie dog, deer, and pronghorn. When human hunters eliminated its prey, the coyote became a semi-scavenger like the jackal.

The coyote now eats mostly small animals and carrion, and also fruit, tubers, and plants when it is very hungry. In rural settings it preys on small pets.

Coyotes usually live alone or in pairs, and both parents help rear the young. Coyotes, much like wolves, use eerie howling to communicate and feces and urine to mark territory.

The Navaho people of North America have many stories and legends in which the Coyote is a recurring figure. Coyote is a master trickster from whom not even the gods are safe. During the creation when the night sky was made, instead of carefully placing all the stars, Coyote just haphazardly flung them in one mass and created the Milky Way.

Ornaments made in the likeness of
the wolf keep bad luck from entering
the house. It is considered good luck
to have a wolf cross your path.

Wolf

At last we come to the wolf, *Canis lupus*, the largest member of the Canidae. There are three wolf species (Gray Wolf, Red Wolf, and Ethiopian Wolf), with thirty-two subspecies of the present-day wolf recorded worldwide. Some may reach 31 inches (77.5cm) at the shoulders, 4.5 feet (1.5m) in length (not including the tail), and weigh as much as 175 pounds (79kg).

Wolves are extremely adaptable and can live in both grasslands and open woods. Although wolves are powerful enough to take large musk oxen and caribou, they prefer the smaller deer, wild sheep, and goats. Wolves are intelligent hunters and whenever it is possible, they choose prey that is more easily brought down—younger, older, and/or weaker animals. Wolves also may run alongside their prey, slashing and tearing at it until the victim is weakened enough to be killed. One wolf may grab the prey by the nose and hang on, while others close in for the kill. Sometimes wolves drive an animal in relays until it falls from exhaustion, or they may herd an unwary victim into the jaws of waiting associates.

Wolves are true pack animals, living and hunting in extended family groups consisting of father, mother, and pups from both the current and previous years. In lean years, several families may band together and form packs of a dozen members or more. Wolves establish their territory by scent-marking and howling, and a rigid social order is maintained within the pack. Wolves normally mate for life, and both parents care for pups. Often, the death of one of a "married" pair of wolves may be followed by the death (from sadness?) of the other, even if the remaining partner is healthy.

Wolves are the domestic dog's closest wild relative. Scientists believe that the smallest, the Asiatic Wolf, *Canis lupus pallipes*, shown here, was a likely first forebear. Even today, many of the northern sled dog breeds retain a distinctive wolfish appearance. When we first domesticated dogs, we invited the wildness of the wolf into the parlor.

By the early sixteenth century (during Henry VII's reign), wolves were extinct in England; they were no longer in existence in Scotland by the eighteenth century, but according to legend, may have lingered until 1848; they disappeared from Ireland in 1821. The last Japanese wolf was reported in 1904. Today in North America, although endangered, protected wolves have made a comeback.

Just listen to the fervent yapping of the diminutive Chihuahua or the baleful baying of the Bloodhound; watch the Greyhound's graceful sprint and the Pomeranian's mincing step; feel the Bulldog's wet snuffling kiss; thrill to the uncanny howls of the Malamute. No matter the wrapping, it's obvious that beneath the fur lies the heart and soul of the wolf.

Similarities between the social behavior of wolves and humans have
resulted in the many stories of children being raised by wolves. One
of the most famous of these myths celebrates Romulus and Remus,
brothers who later founded Rome.

Humans have long watched and envied the hunting prowess of the wolf. The ancient Greeks considered Apollo a wolf-god, and the Arcadians worshiped Zeus as a wolf-god. Norsemen sought to capture the wolf's skill through the magic of naming. Beowulf (War Wolf) may be one of the most famous examples, and even the ships of the Norsemen were called "sea wolves."

CANID CLASSIFICATION

GENUS *CANIS*
Side-striped Jackal, *Canis adustus*
Golden Jackal, *Canis aureus*
Black-backed Jackal, *Canis mesolmelas*
Simenian Jackal, *Canis simensis*
Dingo, *Canis dingo*
Domestic dog, *Canis familiaris*
Coyote, *Canis latrans*
Artic Wolf, *Canis lupus arctos*
Eastern Wolf, *Canis lupus lycaon*
Ethiopian Wolf, *Canis simensis*
Gray Wolf, *Canis lupus*
Himalayan Wolf, *Canis himalayensis*
Indian (Asiatic) Wolf, *Canis lupis pallipes*
Red Wolf, *Canis rufus*

GENUS *VULPES*
Bengali Fox, *Vulpes bengalensis*
Southwest Asian or Banford's Fox, *Vulpes canus*
Cape Silver Fox, *Vulpes chama*
Gray Fox, *Vulpes cinereoargentatus*

Corsac Fox, *Vulpes corsac*
Tibetan Sand Fox, *Vulpes ferrilatus*
Indian Desert Fox, *Vulpes leucopus*
Pale Fox, *Vulpes pallida*
Sand Fox, *Vulpes ruppelli*
Swift or Kit Fox, *Vulpes velox*
Red Fox, *Vulpes vulpes*

GENUS *DUSICYON* (SOUTH AMERICAN CANIDS)
Zorro, *Dusicyon culpaeolus*
Culpeo Fox, *Dusicyon culpaeus*
Zorro, *Dusicyon fulvipes*
Pampas Fox, *Dusicyon griseus*
Zorro, *Dusicyon gymnocercus*
Inca Fox, *Dusicyon inca*
Zorro, *Dusicyon sechurae*
Zorro, *Dusicyon vetulus*

GENUS *ALOPEX*
Arctic Fox, *Alopex lagopus*

GENUS *ATELOCYNUS*
Zorro, *Ateiocynus microtus*

GENUS *CERDOCYON*
Crab-eating Fox, *Cerdocyon thous*

GENUS *CHRYSOCYON*
Maned Wolf, *Chrysocyon brachyurus*

GENUS *CUON*
Dhole, *Cuon alpinus*

GENUS *FENNECUS*
Fennec, *Fennecus zerda*

GENUS *LYCAON*
African Painted Dog, *Lycaon pictus*

GENUS *NYCTEREUTES*
Raccoon Dog, *Nyctereutes procyonoides*

GENUS *OTOCYON*
Bat-eared Fox, *Otocyon megalotis*

GENUS *SPEOTHOS*
Bush Dog, *Speothos venaticus*

The Egyptian god Anubis looks similar to several modern-day canid species, and dog breeds.

FROM WOLF TO WHELP

How did early man and the wolf get together? About 100,000 years ago, humans and wolves were probably rarely in direct competition for food. In the northern regions of Eurasia, humans concentrated on hunting woolly mammoth and rhinoceros, while wolves preferred smaller prey. Wolves didn't become important to people until the decline and extinction of the big, slow-moving game. Then humans were forced to turn to much fleeter, smaller prey, and became direct rivals of the wolves.

It's hard to ascertain exactly how our early ancestors hunted, but more than likely they were as aggressive as their wolf competitors. It's reasonable to assume the wolf was domesticated not by design, but for mutual benefit. Humans admired the wolf's ability to scent track, and wolves enjoyed leftovers of the human hunt.

Primal human and wolf societies were very similar: both were composed of relatively small units, were capable of hunting larger game either in the open or wooded areas, and utilized team effort. In addition, human hunter-gatherers and wolf packs shared food with weaker non-hunting members of the group, like wolf pups or human infants. Very probably, humans also noticed that the howling of the wolves paralleled their own vocal communication.

Archeological evidence shows that Stone Age humans often killed entire herds of animals, stampeding them with fire until they became mired in mud, or were driven off cliffs. Only a few animals were eaten, while the rest were left to rot. Early humans were surely in awe of the wolf's ability to determine weak members of the herd and "cut" them out for the kill; such ability proved useful to humans. During the Mesolithic period (about 20,000 to 10,000 years ago) hunters seem to have selected good herders from the wolves following them.

Wolf pups in the wild participate in wolf society; when raised with humans, they transfer this affection to men

NEOTENY

The retention of infantile behavioral characteristics, such as barking, is apparent in almost all domestic dogs. This is a distinct difference between wild and domesticated canids. Such puppyish appearance or behavior in adults is called "neoteny."

Most domesticated dogs are "lop-eared," with the ears hanging limply over their cheeks. Even straight eared breeds like the German Shepherd retain floppy ears through much of puppyhood. All wild canids have erect ears from shortly after birth on.

The curved (or sickle) tail is another sign of neoteny. Wild canid puppies carry their tails spiked straight up, but wild adults always hold their tails at a downward angle when not using them to communicate. Compare this with the tails of nearly all domestic adult dogs, which curve up even when the dog is at rest.

and women. The first wolf cub adopted into human society would likely have assumed that it was a hairy human—or that its companions were hairless wolves—and enthusiastically treated the humans as members of its pack.

Dogs may have diverged from wolves much earlier than previously thought, and in multiple locations. In 2008, a team of scientists at Goyet Cave (Belgium) identified a dog that lived 36,000 years ago. They believe the Aurignacian people of Europe (during the Upper Paleolithic period) first domesticated dogs. The second oldest known dog, found in the Altai Mountains of Siberia in 1975, dates to 33,000 B.P. based on DNA analysis published in 2013. Robert Wayne's team (University of California, Los Angeles) compared wolf and dog DNA and believes the two diverged 50,000 years ago in North Africa or Egypt rather than East Asia as previously thought.

The "polar" or "spitz" dog breeds are among the earliest of the modern dogs. They seem closest to their wolf cousins and originally shared the ranges of nomadic people living within the Arctic Circle. *Canis familiaris palustris*, or the Peat Dog, appeared during the Neolithic Age (6000 or 5000 B. C.) and managed to spread across Europe. The Peat Dog was sized midway

Ancient cultures recognized and admired the hunting prowess of wolves, which figured prominently in their legends and myths. Wolf-cults adopted the wolf as a totem and imitated wolf behavior. The ancient Celts believed the horned nature-god Cernunnos was often accompanied by a wolf. The wolf also accompanied Odin, chief god of the Norse pantheon, and the Norse underworld boasted a god known as Fenris-wolf. Fenris-wolf symbolized chaos and the everlasting ice fields that would one day return to engulf the world. Perhaps this story derived from some primal memory of man roaming the ice floes in the company of wolves.

between the jackal and fox, and possessed a tapering muzzle, a wide, deep chest, and slight legs. The Peat Dog would probably look similar to a modern-day Samoyed. Today's polar dogs include Huskies, Malamutes, Norwegian Elkhounds, and others.

The Dingo of Australia and the Pariah Dog of southern Asia and northern Africa are very similar ancient dog types. Both are short-haired, medium-size dogs with curled tails; their coats come in a variety of colors.

Gazehounds and sight-hunting dogs were probably bred from Dingo-Pariah stock selected for speed crossing open country. Gazehounds vary in coat color and length, but are almost uniformly long-legged, narrow-headed, and lightly built. The Saluki of Asia Minor may be the most ancient existing purebred today. Other gazehounds include the Borzoi, Collie, Whippet, and Afghan Hound. From the early sighthound, and Pariah types sprang the varieties of today's breeds.

The first noticeable changes in tamed wolves reflecting domesticity are a foreshortening of the muzzle, crowding of the tooth rows, and a comparative overall reduction in tooth size. The teeth of modern dogs haven't changed very much from those of their ancestors 30 thousand years ago; based upon a single tooth, it's hard to tell if a canid fossil belonged to an early dog or came instead from a local wild species of wolf. Some of the earliest "short-faced" wolves that crossed the border between wildness and domestication were animals larger than, but otherwise much resembling modern Eskimo dogs.

Exactly when did the wolf shed its wild ways and become a dog? That question continues to baffle experts and will probably never be satisfactorily resolved. Whatever the answer, it matters little to the dogs of today, or to the humans who love them. Suffice it to say that dogs and people have been enriching each others' lives for eons. Ancient peoples considered wolves "four-legged humans," and surely our present-day dogs can be considered no less. Dog and human are in many ways two sides of the same coin, each so much a part of the other's life that a separate existence is no longer conceivable.

Clay Aboriginal figure portraying a Dingo.

HISTORY OF THE DOG

People have long bred dogs for a variety of uses. But where did the first dogs appear? Domesticated dogs probably originated in Mesopotamia; from there, they gradually spread throughout Asia and Europe. But a nearly parallel, simultaneous development of the human/dog partnership is found in almost every civilization of the world.

The Americas

In North America, the earliest dogs were found at Jaguar Cave, Idaho, carbon-dated 9500 to 8400 B.C. In 1921, two dog mummies of Basket Maker Dogs were discovered at White Dog Cave in Arizona. These date from around the birth of Christ. Both were found with fur-robe-wrapped human mummies.

Two types of dogs were common to ancient Mexico. The first served as beloved companions and were very similar to the Chihuahua we know today. The other was medium size with brown markings and looked something like the early Egyptian and Greek dogs (similar to modern Dalmatians).

The Aztec civilization of Old Mexico occupied an ecosystem lacking large mammals suitable for food. Aztecs instead ate ducks, turkeys, and a wide assortment of domestic dogs similar to the bald Xoloitzcuintli or Mexican Hairless.

European dogs were brought to the New World by Christopher Columbus during his second voyage. Those twenty dogs originally served as food tasters. They were also used to hunt game and were themselves eaten when game was scarce. The Native Americans held great fear of these ferocious "devouring dogs" and they were instrumental in the victory of the Conquistadors.

The *moneria infernal* (infernal hunt) offered pleasures for the Spanish conquerors, who considered the locals little more than animals. Dogs were used to punish and terrorize in organized spectacles in which they were pitted against one or even groups of unarmed Native Americans. In this way, the young dogs were trained to attack and devour.

Egypt

Dogs have been bred in the Middle East since at least 4000 B.C. Egyptian murals show many types of sighthounds; these dogs were very successful in desert countries where the hot, still air made scenting difficult but allowed excellent visibility. Some dogs had upright bat-ears like the modern Ibizan Hound, while others had small drop-ears with the feathering of the Saluki.

Dogs often appeared in Egyptian art. Hunting scenes in the tomb of Tiy, wife of Amenhotep III (1417-1379 B.C.) show various domestic types ranging from the Greyhound to the spitz. A wooden casket in the Cairo museum shows Pharaoh Tutankhamen (1370-1352 B.C.) standing upright in his chariot shooting arrows at enemy soldiers while his cream-colored, spike-collared Mastiff dogs attack them.

Later pharaohs preferred cats for hunting in the marshes but also continued to use the Greyhound for hunting antelope. A Dalmatian-type dog eventually took the place of the Greyhound. The Pharaoh Hound partnered with cats to protect grain from rodents. Pictures in tombs at Beni Hasan, Egypt, show it to have changed little in 2,000 years.

Although early Egyptians worshipped cats, they adored dogs as well. About 4240 B.C. the upper Egyptian culture worshipped Set, a Greyhound figure with a forked tail. Never considered subordinates by the Egyptians, dogs served as hunters, war dogs, even temple dogs, but always equals. Killing a dog was punishable by death. Only slaves or children acted as shepherds of livestock, an occupation considered too lowly for the dog. After death, the dog was embalmed, and its remains were placed in a sarcophagus; the dog's human family mourned its passing with weeping and by shaving their entire bodies.

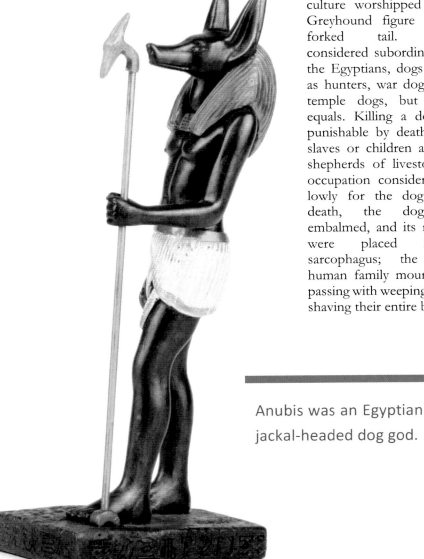

Anubis was an Egyptian jackal-headed dog god.

(Left, previous page) Pre-Columbian dog vase made around 1200 A.D.

Ancient Greece and Rome

The dog of Greece was both a warrior/hunter and a guardian of the flock and house. Early Assyrian wall paintings (c. 625 B.C.) show large, heavy Mastiff-like dogs with wrinkled heads and curled tails apparently used for hunting wolves and lions. These dogs were treasured and bred by Greeks who called them Molossians, and the Romans gave the group its modern name of Mastiff (from *mansuetus*, or "tame," referring to their use as family guard dogs). Alexander the Great (356-323 B.C.) was so fond of a Mastiff-type dog given to him by the king of Albania that he had a whole town built in its memory. By the time of Christ, Mastiffs were common in much of the civilized world.

Overall, the Greeks weren't terribly concerned with dogs. Plutarch says dogs were not tolerated in Athens, and a Roman priest who stroked a dog had to purify himself before he could take part in any sacrifices. Statues of the physician Hippocrates (460—377 B.C.) often depicted him with a snake beneath his feet and a dog at his side, symbolizing the common fatal afflictions of the time: poison and rabies.

In Rome, owning dogs was a privilege of the leisure class, and it was fashionable to keep dogs in the house. Less-monied folk made do with geese as household guardians. Dogs were also used for communications. These dogs were made to swallow metal tubes containing secret messages; upon delivery, the dogs were sacrificed to recover the message.

The citadel of Corinth was guarded by fifty dogs. One night, the dogs defended Corinth from a surprise attack, and all were killed but one. The lone survivor ran back to the fortress to raise the alarm and managed to save the city. In gratitude, a marble monument to the memory of the brave dogs was erected. The surviving dog, named Soter, was given a pension for life and a solid silver collar inscribed, "To Soter, defender and savior of Corinth, placed under the protection of his friends."

The Romans starved their war-trained "devouring dogs" for several days before combat to make them more ferocious. Roman war Mastiffs often wore their own armor, with leather-mounted knives fixed to collars, backs, and sides to damage the enemy's legs and horses. Dogs fitted with torches frightened the horses and disrupted enemy cavalry charges. Mastiffs also attacked and frightened elephants that carried archers in classical times.

Persia

Early Persians treasured dogs for their work as shepherd of the flocks and protector of humans. It was considered a crime to kill dogs and a duty to cherish them, according to the decree of Ormuzd, the Son of Fire. Ancient Persians called their great and wise men Khan (the Dog), which symbolized gentleness and wisdom.

The Persian kings also used ferocious dogs for war. Cyrus the Great released four towns in Babylon from taxes in exchange for breeding and training combat Mastiffs for his army. Mastiffs continued to be used as war animals into the sixteenth century; Henry VIII of England beat Charles V of Germany by sending 500 starving dogs into battle.

A custom of early Persians required delaying the burial of close relatives of their seers until the dead body was ripped apart by wild beasts. The great Roman statesman Cicero (106-43 B.C.) wrote in Book One of *The Tusculan* that poor people in Persia used the village's stray dogs to do so, while richer folk used their own household dogs.

The ancestors of today's Pariah Dogs were probably shepherds forsaken when herding was abandoned. Today in India, Pariah Dogs commonly devour garbage and corpses, and are often offered water because of their good work as cleansers of the streets.

Moslems have traditionally regarded the dog as unclean. Islamic legend holds a dog guilty of devouring the body of Mohammed, and tradition has demanded that dogs be hanged in the streets as punishment for the crime.

(Above) Hare hunting in Algeria, 1860.

(Below) Gazelle hunting in Persia with Kurdish Greyhounds and falcon.

Among the pantheon of early Japan was Omisto, the god of suicide. Omisto had the body of a man with head of a dog and rode a charger with seven heads. Omisto promised eternal joy to any man who killed himself in Omisto's honor.

Eastern Asia

About 3468 B.C., Fo-Hi of China encouraged the breeding of tiny "Sleeve Dogs." The Chinese in A.D. 100 were breeding "Pai Dogs," which were short-legged, short-mouthed dogs that "belonged under the table."

The Shih Tzu (Son of Lion) has been bred since A.D. 624. China also produced the Pug, introduced to Europe by traders of The Dutch East India Company in the seventeenth century. But the most ancient dwarf dog, called "Little Lion-Dog" or "Butterfly-Lion" is the Pekingese, dating from at least 3,000 years ago.

Dog meat was often part of royal banquets, served alongside roast beef, pork, and ram. Chow Chows represent selective breeding of polar-type dogs, and were used both for food and as temple guards.

The early Pekingese were so dwarfed and twisted that stunted jaws made it impossible for them to eat normal food. As a result, the babies of slave girls were killed, and the dogs fed by nursing from the childless women.

The Celts who settled in Gaul (France) in fifth century B.C. followed a Gallic religion in which their god Smertulus was the "devouring dog," a symbol of destruction and death.

Europe: The Dog in Disfavor

The Middle Ages were centuries of turmoil for Europeans, but more so for their dogs. Countless dogs followed soldiers and were abandoned all along their travels. Ownerless dogs wandered the cities, living on garbage, and banded together to scavenge the countryside. Those that survived quickly reverted to a semi-wild state and copied their ancestors' proclivity for digging up and feeding upon corpses.

Only the wealthy minority could afford to keep dogs. The rest of the populace saw only the terrifying packs of scavenging wild dogs, which filled them with superstitious fear. Many peasants readily believed the legends of fantastical creatures. Devil dogs, werewolves,

dog-headed dragons, and other hideous canine creatures leered from church architecture as gargoyles and flourished in the imagination of the people. The words "dog" and "cur" became curses. The Catholic Church's Second Council of Macon (A.D. 585) forbade priests from having dogs guard their houses "as much because of the noise and salacious behavior of these animals, as because of the poison [possibly rabies] which is transmitted in their bite."

Inadvertently, the cat saved the dog from continued vilification; the cat was guilty of having been made a god in Egypt. When the church turned its attention to eradicating "feline evil," the dog was reinstated as companion and faithful servant.

WEREWOLVES!

Werewolf lore (lycanthropy) reflects man's fear of the wolf's powers, and perhaps, of his own capacity for savagery. Werewolf scares occurred quite frequently during medieval times, and werewolf hangings were common; the afflicted human supposedly reverted to wolf form at death. Wolf cults prospered for some time during the Christianization of Europe.

In 1685 in Germany, a dead burgomaster was said to have ravaged the countryside as a werewolf. The unpopular King John of England was also reputed to have become a werewolf after he died. In those days, anyone with physical peculiarities such as extreme hairiness or eyebrows that grew across their brow, was suspect.

THE CELEBRATED DOG

In England and Europe, wealthy nobles maintained packs of hounds for stag, wolf, or boar hunting, and imposed laws and penalties for the protection of their dogs. Monasteries began breeding dogs and trying to create new specialized breeds for the nobility. The first was the Saint Hubert Hound, produced by the monks of the Abbey of Saint-Hubert at Mouzon in the Ardennes in the eighth century. Given as a gift to the king of France, this valuable Bloodhound became quite common in less than twenty-five years. From these first Bloodhounds were derived a vast array of scent hounds, from giant to miniature.

Nobles often purchased dogs at inflated prices, trying to improve their lines. During his travels, King Louis IX of France (1226-1270) brought back the grey dogs (gazehounds) with which he had hunted gazelle in the Holy Land. Crossbreeding these dogs with existing breeds created a number of new specialty dogs: large Wolfhounds and Mastiffs for hunting bear or wild boar, smaller dogs to flush birds, and setters to drive game into nets. Soon, the right to hunt became reserved as a privilege of class. No longer a means of obtaining food, hunting became a sport.

1863 French dog exposition (dog show).

Hunting dogs were prized and pampered. Eventually this "harmless" pastime of princes and kings began to bother the Church. Noblemen presented themselves for Mass with their hounds at their feet. When reproached for bringing dogs into the church, the hunters refused to be separated from their furry companions, and heard Mass outside, with all the church doors open. Indeed, Charles IX of France (1550—1574) was so fond of "Courte," a white water retriever called a Griffon, that he allowed her to eat from his own plate. When she died, he had a pair of gloves made from her hide to keep her near him.

In 1576, France's annual budget for royal dogs reached 100,000 gold crowns. Henry III (1551-1589) often appeared for the most serious occasions wearing a ribbon-trimmed basket hung from his neck in which rested several little dogs (Papillons).

The monarch William the Conqueror who lived 1028-1087 demanded every dog not belonging to him should have three toes cut off to slow its speed. King Francis I of France (1494-1547) decreed, "All dogs belonging to peasant or farmer must wear, attached to their necks, a heavy block of wood, the weight and bulkiness of which will stem their ardor, whenever they move away from their homes. If despite this precaution they take to hunting on royal land they will be punished... by hamstringing...." And Henry III of England (1551-1589) issued an edict in 1578 barring commoners from hunting, upon pain of death.

The modern Afghan Hound looks similar to ancient sighthounds.

Small dogs were no less prized. Terriers originally served alongside ferrets to kill rats. The ferrets were released down burrows to "flush" rats to the surface, where the dogs would kill them, a sport known as "ratting." A fifteenth-century cartoon even shows terriers chasing rats in a hospital ward. A good ratting terrier killed hundreds of rodents a day.

According to The Guinness Book of Records, a Bull Terrier named Jenny Lind once killed 500 rats in 1.5 hours. By the end of the Middle Ages, the dog's position had transformed from a source of fear and hostility to that of privileged hunter. With the advent of the Renaissance, the dog became a friend as well.

THE RENAISSANCE DOG

In this time of prosperity and plenty in Europe, dogs were kept by the wealthy, the working class, and even farmers. Dogs of all shapes and sizes were everywhere. Mastiffs rode beside wealthy Italian citizens. At court and in castles all over the continent, the ladies pampered miniatures of hounds and bushy dogs.

The sport of "baiting" became popular. From the thirteenth century on, dogs in England were cruelly pitted against each other or other animals for the pleasure of human observers. Bulldogs and Bull Terriers originally produced for cattle management at the butchers proved ideal. Their aggressiveness and tenacity made them well suited for the bloody sport of baiting. Not all dogs had it so rough, though. Some were performers or workers that turned spits in kitchens; others filled more traditional roles as sheepdogs.

By the eighteenth century, pampered lap dogs became the rage. Pugs, Papillons, and Maltese had their fur cropped and crimped to match their mistress' hairstyle of the day. But hunting dogs remained the pampered pooch of choice. They ate with their masters and often slept in their bedrooms.

The French Revolution and the fall of the monarchy (1792) brought an end to privilege of rank in France and hunting finally was permitted for commoners. Pedigreed dogs bred for pack hunting with horses became obsolete, and the Napoleonic wars and social unrest ended the lines of many breeds. English breeders concentrated on perfecting a gun-dog, and the setter was developed. From this dog came the Pointer, shown for the first time in France in 1860.

RECENT HISTORY

By 1851, for the first time in England's history, more than half the population lived in urban areas. The expanding middle classes and their rising social aspirations caused an unprecedented demand for luxury. Owning a dog was the epitome of refinement.

In England, the Royal Society for the Prevention of Cruelty to Animals (RSPCA) formed in 1837, with the Australian branch opening in 1871. The American SPCA was founded in 1866, the American Humane Association in 1877, and the Toronto Humane Society in 1887. Veterinary medicine made great strides during those years.

Dogs owe a debt of gratitude to Louis Pasteur (1870—1914), who finally perfected a vaccine against the dreaded rabies. In 1920, a diabetic dog was saved by insulin for the first time at the University of Toronto. Once anesthetics were perfected, surgeries to correct all sorts of ailments became available, and veterinary medicine began to flourish.

Interest in breeding new varieties and refining old breeds persisted well into the nineteenth century. The great hunting dogs and pack hounds were already listed in "stud books" of ancestry. With the first dog show in 1859 in England, fanciers wanted to establish the lines of other breeds. The Kennel Club in Britain formed in 1873. Similar organizations soon followed around the world.

Today, people continue to perfect and redefine all kinds of dogs. Breed clubs have standardized many breeds and keep meticulous records of bloodlines. There are more than 250 different dog breeds officially recognized around the world.

The category of working dogs isn't necessarily of specific breeds. Service dogs have been around for centuries, too, with guide dogs for the blind commonly depicted in Medieval art and writing. Possibly the earliest depiction of a guide dog leading a blind person is on a surviving fresco of Pompei (79 CE). Today, guide and signal dogs, bomb- and drug-sniffing dogs, search-and-rescue, medical alert dogs and other service dogs may be a variety of purebreds, or even mixes. You name the task, and a dog will do it.

It is the generic "pet dog" that has outdistanced all others in popularity. Today, the U.S. has the greatest number of pet dogs at 79 million, followed by China (27.4 million), Russia (12.5 million), Japan (12 million), and Great Britain (9 million). Whether pampered purebreds or cherished mixes, their work as companions has brought them closer to humans than at any time in the past. Truly the dog is *Canis fidelis*—faithful dog.

> Outside of a dog, a book is man's best friend. Inside a dog, it's too dark to read.
>
> --Groucho Marx

Two:
Cultured Canine

CANINE LITERATURE

The dog has inspired artists for centuries. Writers have celebrated the dog's love, devotion, and steadfast loyalty perhaps more than that of any other animal. Many authors express a profound passion for the dog, and it is obvious that the feeling is mutual.

The classical poet Homer, who lived in Ancient Greece about the ninth century B.C., was probably the first to introduce the dog in literature. In the Odyssey, Homer tells the moving tale of Argus, the faithful, beloved dog of Ulysses. Abandoned, starving, and scorned by his master's friends, Argus pathetically dragged himself about the streets until Ulysses finally returned to Ithaca after twenty years. Argus died of happiness at finding his master once more.

The Greek philosopher Aristotle (384-322 B.C.) was another early author who wrote fondly of the dog. He praised the courage of the Laconian Mastiffs and listed the most useful breeds of the time. The Roman poet Virgil (70-19 B.C.) wrote of the great debt owed to the swift Bloodhounds of Sparta. Both the scholar Varro of Rome (116-27 B.C.) and later, the poet Ovid (43 B.C. to A.D. 16) described the best dogs to own, and where to find them.

The Roman scholar Pliny the Elder (A.D. 23-79) held forth on the affections of the dog, and even wrote a natural history that included the dog. Arrien (second century) wrote a work regarded as an authority for centuries on the 1,000 secrets of hunting with dogs. The

Greek fabulist Aesop attributed to the dog all the virtues and vices of a human. His fable of the dog sleeping in the ox's hay is probably the source of the term "dog in the manger," referring to a selfish person who jealously guards something from others even though it may be useless to himself.

Literature is filled with authors that either adore and celebrate the dog, or ridicule and despise it. The saying *Qui me amat, amat et canem meum* ("Love me, love my dog") is credited to St. Bernard of Clairvaux, a French clergyman who lived during the twelfth century. The English poet Geoffrey Chaucer (1342-1400) was the first to say, "It is nought good a slepyng hound to wake."

Writers of the Middle Ages often made the lowly dog the butt of pointed political and moral barbs. Jean La Fontaine (1621-1695), a French poet, seemed to take particular pleasure demeaning the dog. Although he acknowledged the dog to be a symbol of duty and devotion, he believed the dog stupid and greedy, overflowing with shortcomings. In "The Wolf and Dog," La Fontaine writes contemptuously of the "willing slavishness" of the dog compared to the freedom of a wolf, which would rather starve than wear a collar. In his fable "The Dog and Master's Dinner," the dog spinelessly shares his master's meal with three other dogs rather than defend it in the face of sure defeat: "An excess of devotion is not worth fighting for."

Popular opinion during the Middle Ages held the dog in contempt. Rabies presented a very real threat and masses of abandoned dogs roaming and scavenging for their existence did little to better a seedy reputation. The very word "dog" came to mean a worthless or inferior person; the expression "dog-eat-dog" probably referred to

the sorry strays that were marked by a ruthless, competitive self-interest, which was the quality that allowed them to survive. To "dog it" meant to be a shirker; to "go to the dogs" was to fall into ruin; a "dog's

chance" was almost no chance and to lead a "dog's life" was to have a miserable, dismal existence.

My profits have gone to the dogs,
My trade has been such a deceiver,
I fear that my aim
Is a mere losing game,
Unless I can find a Retriever.

Thomas Hood (1799-1845)
Dog-grel Verses

Even literature had its own doggy pejorative. "Doggerel" was a type of comic or burlesque verse considered trivial and inferior.

The Renaissance saw the revival of interest in art and science, and an ability to appreciate and utilize the dog as never before. In the twelfth century, an English Franciscan monk named Bartholomew Ganville had published a book on animal medicine which became widely read only now. The renewed interest in the dog led to the publication of several such books, including George Turberville's treatise *The Selection, Hygiene and Illnesses of the Dog*.

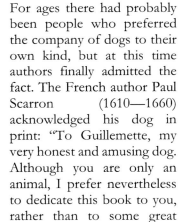

For ages there had probably been people who preferred the company of dogs to their own kind, but at this time authors finally admitted the fact. The French author Paul Scarron (1610—1660) acknowledged his dog in print: "To Guillemette, my very honest and amusing dog. Although you are only an animal, I prefer nevertheless to dedicate this book to you, rather than to some great satrap whose sleep I would thereby be troubling."

Still, some men of science divorced themselves from the emotional attachment to dogs. For example, the philosopher Rene Descartes (1596-1650) believed the dog nothing but a piece of machinery, lacking feelings

(Above) Roman floor mosaic of hunting dogs.

or emotions; his colleague Blaise Pascal (1623-1662) shared Descartes' scorn for the dog. But not everyone agreed with these great men. The Marquise de Sevigne (1626-1696) responded, "Machines which love, which prefer one person to another, machines which are jealous... come now! Descartes never thought to make us believe that!" The English poet William Blake (1757-1827) even compared the treatment a man gave his dog to the country's social health: "A dog starved at his master's gate/ Predicts the ruin of the state."

As the dog's popularity increased, so did its defenders. The French fabulist Florian (1755-1794), like Aesop and La Fontaine before him, used fables featuring animals to prove points, but he treated the dog with more sympathy. In "La Brebis et le Chien" ("The Sheep and the Dog"), the sheep tempts the dog to join him in a revolt against the cruelties of man. But the dog wisely refuses, noting that it's always better "to submit to evil rather than to do evil."

During the Romanticism of the eighteenth century, it became quite acceptable to express one's feelings for pets. By the nineteenth century, the dog was perceived as "Faithful Fido," staunch defender and companion of man. Writers celebrated the dog in romantic, sentimental poetry. In 1844, Elizabeth Barrett Browning (1806-1861) wrote a tender tribute to her dog, "Flush":

...Therefore to this dog will I,
Tenderly not scornfully,
Render praise and favor

Alphonse de Lamartine (1790-1869) was a French poet who kept and loved dogs. He wrote in "Le chien du solitaire" ("The Lonely Man's Dog"):

Never have I kicked you in scorn,
Never with a brutal word saddened
your tender love,
My heart has never repulsed your
touching caress
But always... Ah, always in you I honor
The ineffable goodness of your Master
and mine.

"The friendship of a dog is without a doubt more intense and more constant than that of a man."

Michel de Montaigne (1533-1592)

Other renowned poets to embrace the dog in their work include the American Robert Frost (1874-1963), Hartley Coleridge (1796-1849), and Scot Robert Burns (1759-1796). Even American songwriter Stephen Foster (1826—1864) honored the dog in his song "Old Dog Tray." Later, the English poet A.A. Milne (1882—1956) and the American Odgen Nash (1902-1971) poked gentle fun at the dog in humorous verse.

Epitaphs for beloved dogs were a favorite literary form of many writers. Sir Walter Scott (1771-1832) built a marble mausoleum at his house at Abbotsford, Scotland to the memory of Maida, a Scottish Deerhound. It bore the inscription *Sit tibi terra levis* ("May the earth lie lightly on you"). Scott said of the dog, "Recollect that the Almighty, who gave the dog to be companion of our pleasure and our toils, hath invested him a nature noble and incapable of deceit."

Sculpture of Russian short story writer and playwright Anton Chekov (1860-1904), with his dog.

The English poet Lord Byron (1788-1824) owed his life to a Newfoundland dog named Boatswain, which found him when he was lost and injured as a child. In 1808, he erected a monument to Boatswain with the following inscription: "Near this spot are deposited the remains of one who possessed beauty without vanity, strength without insolence, courage without ferocity, and all the virtues of Man, without his vices. This praise, which would be unmeaning flattery if inscribed over human ashes, is but a just tribute to the memory of Boatswain, a dog."

As the nineteenth century progressed, the perception of dogs became less cliched, and a variety of noble, wicked, and commonplace dogs were represented in literature. The French writer Victor Hugo (1802-1885) adored dogs and wrote about those that shared his life.

Apparently, dogs loved him as well. A Poodle he gave to a diplomat living in Moscow ran away, and within a few months found its way back to Paris and was discovered scratching at Hugo's door.

The English novelist Charles Dickens (1812-1870) celebrated the dog in countless books and stories, describing Bouncer the Pomeranian, Don the Newfoundland, and Sultan the hunting dog in *My Father as I Recall Him*. The French author and artist Jean Cocteau (1889-1963) wrote and illustrated the book *Un drole de menage* (*A Strange Family*). In it, a couple named Lord Sun and Lady Moon were too busy to properly raise their children, who became cruel, stupid, and wicked as a result. The pet dog was then entrusted with raising the children, and taught them to be good, patient, and obedient.

The English author Rudyard Kipling (1865-1936) was a dog lover, who said of his Cocker Spaniel, "He is my most sincere admirer; he loves me though he has never read my work!" Toward the end of Kipling's life he wrote the story "Thy Servant a Dog," and in his poem "The Power of the Dog," Kipling warns of the pain that is sure to follow if one loves a dog too much—for the dog will die, and its owner will be left bereft: "Brothers and Sisters, I bid you beware/ Of giving your heart to a dog to tear."

Dogs have been featured frequently in American literature as well, from their roles as hunting dogs in William Faulkner's novels to background characters in stories of the frontier. Dogs set the scene in Mark Twain's *Huckleberry Finn*, in which the "loafers" of the village delight in their cruelty to stray dogs. Twain seemed touched by the plight of the dog. Even his short stories dealt with the sorry reality of the dog's life. In "A Dog's Tale," a brave little dog is rewarded for her heroism and courage by having her puppy selfishly sacrificed to prove a meaningless point, whereupon she dies of sorrow.

Stephen Crane's short story, "A Dark-Brown Dog" gives another evocative example of a dog's life. "Down in the mystic, hidden fields of his little dog-soul bloomed flowers of love and fidelity and perfect faith."

Zane Grey (1872-1939), whose novels about the American West remain very popular, enjoyed hunting and the companionship of dogs. Of the more than forty dogs to have appeared in his stories, many were victims of the unthinking cruelty of men who considered dogs a mere tool. In real life, Grey loved and kept many dogs; two favorites were an Airedale and a Paiute Shepherd. The Paiute was even mentioned in the novel *Stranger from the Tonto*. The story of Don, a tale about a brave hound that hunted lions, was based on fact; however, although the Don of the story never came back, the real-life Don did return from his adventures. Hunting dogs have been not only sources of pride for their masters, but also well-loved companions.

Jack London (1876-1916) has stirred the emotions of dog lovers for generations with his stories of the sled dogs of the icy North. One of his best-known novels is *The Call of the Wild*. Told by a St. Bernard mix named Buck, the story recounts his kidnapping and life as a sled dog during the Alaskan gold rush. Buck's adventures bring him near death, on to a great love of one man, and eventually to his destiny as the leader of his own pack of wolves.

When I get to heaven, first thing I'll do,
Grab my horn, and I'll blow for Old Blue.
Saying, "Come on, Blue, finally got here too."

...from "Old Blue," an American folk song

If you pick up a starving dog and make him prosperous, he will not bite you. This is the principal difference between a dog and a man.

Mark Twain (1835-1920

Albert Payson Terhune (1872-1942), an American journalist, wrote countless dog stories based on the Collies he raised at his Sunnybank Kennels. His first novel *Lad: A Dog* became a bestseller in both adult and young adult fiction. Terhune authored 30 more novels, all featuring Collies, that remain quite popular today.

James Thurber (1894-1961) devoted himself to more humorous aspects of the dog/human relationship. His hilarious story "The Dog That Bit People," from *My Life and Times*, tells of an Airedale named Muggs who bit friend and foe alike. The only thing Muggs feared was thunderstorms so Thurber's mother rigged a "thunder machine" from sheet metal she shook to make Muggs come inside the house. In an introduction to *The Fireside Book of Dog Stories*, Thurber summed up his feelings about dogs: "The dog has got more fun out of Man than Man has got out of the dog, for the clearly demonstrable reason that Man is the more laughable of the two animals."

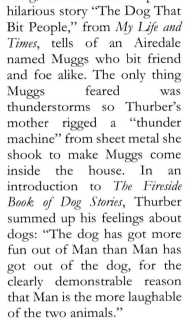

Countless other authors have immortalized the dog, including O. Henry, Don Marquis, Booth Tarkington, and Arthur C. Clarke. Dogs have appeared in all genres, from stories of the past and the plausible to those of horror and the supernatural, as well as uplifting tales set in the future. The incredible dog in Dean Koontz's novel *Watchers* is a product of genetic engineering and amplified canine intelligence. Ray Bradbury tells a chilling tale in "The Emissary"; Stephen King preys on the fears of the past with his mad dog thriller *Cujo*, and his predecessor Fred Gipson evoked similar gooseflesh in the classic *Old Yeller*. Eric Knight's famous story of the loyalty of a Collie in *Lassie Come-Home* continues to enrapture dog lovers.

Today, the dog is celebrated in literature as never before. Countless books, stories, poems, and modern media are devoted solely to the glorification of the dog.

Those who love the dog know the honor is a fitting one; for is it not the dog alone above all others who is called "Man's Best Friend?"

...The one absolutely unselfish friend that a man can have in this selfish world, the one that never deserts him, and the one that never proves ungrateful or treacherous, is his dog...

George Graham Vest, "Tribute to a Dog," 1870

ART OF THE DOG

A painting by Alexandre Gabriel Decamps (1803-60) of Jagdhunde (PD-art)

Our ongoing love affair with dogs was first immortalized in cave drawings. Some of the earliest dog-related treasures were the ancient amulets of the primitive wolf cults. With the advent of classical art in Greece and Rome, the dog began to frequently appear in art. By that time, hunting and family scenes decorated vases; mythical dog-gods and demons figured in murals on tomb walls; even everyday utensils and formal jewelry featured the dog. Massive bronze and stone bas-reliefs and delicate mosaics depicted dogs of war and the hunt, as well as the cherished pet.

The dogs of the Far East, with their massive bodies, Bulldog heads and endearing snub-nose faces, were preserved by sculptors who crafted the ancient Chinese terra-cotta dogs. The famous Korean Dogs of Fo guarded temple doors until about 550 B.C.

During the Middle Ages in Europe, the dog became a popular model, but the open contempt religious authorities held for dogs kept artists wary: they avoided any visual indication of canine intelligence or feelings to keep from offending the Church. The most daring artists showed dogs with aggressive or stupid expressions. When the dog's popularity returned, interpretations became more realistic.

By the fifteenth century, dogs finally began appearing in religious art, but hunting scenes like Jean Fouquet's *Death at Vincennes* remained the most popular treatment. Many other artists included the dog in their work, and Antonio Pisano, known as Pisanello (1395-1455), and Leonardo da Vinci (1452-1579) both made numerous sketches and studies of the dog. At the beginning of the fifteenth century, Greyhounds and Mastiffs were often featured in portraits of the nobility.

Titian's (1488-1576) *Charles V* and Anthony Van Dyck's (1599-1641) *The Family of King Charles I* are classic examples. Peter Paul Rubens (1577-1640) and Diego Velazquez (1599-1660) also portrayed the dog in their works. The depiction of dogs in portraits often offered a subtle commentary on the character of the human subject. If the subject was a bully, his dog might be shown chewing on a bone; if he was a kind, just ruler, a docile, obedient dog would lay at his feet.

Soon, smaller dogs started to appear in art. Francis Clouet (1510-1572) was the first to document the Papillon in his paintings; Paolo Caliari (called Veronese, 1528-1588) painted the Papillon more than any other dog. During the seventeenth and eighteenth centuries, the Dwarf Spaniel of the aristocracy became more noticeable than the hunting dogs of the past. Jean-Honore Fragonard (1732-1806) put Papillon-Spaniels in almost all his paintings, and Thomas Gainsborough (1727-1788) showed for the first time the large, white Pom of "Mrs. Robinson." As the dog became a familiar figure in art, even the common dog began to catch the attention of artists. Pierre Mignard (1612-1695) shows

a dog very similar to today's Brittany. The works of William Hogarth (1697-1794), Antoine Watteau (1684-1721), and Jean-Baptiste Greuze (1725-1805) among others, often included the dog. The painters A. F. Desportes (1661-1743) and Jean-Baptiste Oudry (1686-1755) specialized in painting the dog; Oudry produced a dog catalog of breed studies that has never been matched.

The next century gave rise to romantic paintings of dogs that sought to touch a sentimental chord. Subjects like the old dog pining at his master's grave, or a fat dog begging outside a bakery became the vogue. Alexandre Decamps (1803-1860) painted hounds, poachers' dogs, and the fat town dogs. Henri de Toulouse-Lautrec (1864-1901) painted the strays and street dogs of Paris.

(Above) *The Messenger* (1674 by Jan Verkolje).

(Left) *Alexandra of Denmark* sits with her lap dog. (by Sir Samuel Luke Fildes 1844-1927) (PD-art)

(Above) *Captain Lord George Graham*, in his cabin (William Hogarth, 1697-1764). PD-art

(Left) Bronzes often depicted dogs hunting, in this case attacking a bear.

(Right) Dog bites a dragon, at the Cathedral of Trento, Italy

The German artist Albrecht Durer's (1471—1528) engraving *Saint Eustace* is typical of the symbolic art of the time. (PD-art)

Interior With Dogs (Wouter Verschuur, 1812-74)

It soon became fashionable for gentlemen to pose for portraits in sporting gear with their hunting dogs. Sir Edwin Landseer (1802—1873) was a favorite artist of Queen Victoria and Prince Albert, and he painted the royal family and their dogs. George Earl's early nineteenth-century painting of "Bob" can be found in the Dog Museum in New York. Many of his paintings celebrated the sporting breeds. The English portrait painter Sir Joshua Reynolds (1723-1782) also included portraits of dogs in his work. More recently, painter Jon Van Zyle featured sled dogs in his Alaska scenes. World-renowned photographer William Wegman's (1943-) incredible portraits of his Weimaraner dogs "Man Ray" and "Fay Ray" are quite famous.

Today, dog lovers can choose from a wealth of doggy designs, canine cartoons, and pooch portraits. Prices vary from reasonable to outrageous. There are artists eager to make portraits of your special dog in nearly every medium. But you don't have to commission an artist. You can use a camera to immortalize a favorite friend in your own personal work of art.

(Left) Hunters with dogs (Konopiste Castle, Czech Republic) figure in many sculptures.

(Bottom right) In Roman mythology, Diana was goddess of the hunt, shown here with her coursing hounds.

(Bottom left) Saint Vito Martire, shown below with dogs, is invoked as protection against rabies and animal attacks.

(Left) Illuminated folio: A Hunter and Dogs Pursuing a Fallow Deer (about 1430 -1440) (PD-art)

(Right) Saint Wendelin of Trier (c. 554 - c. 617 AD) is the patron saint of country people and herdsman. He is accompanied by his dog in this stained glass depiction.

SIGN OF THE DOG

The dog represents fidelity, courage, affection, and generosity. The Dukes of Montmorency, Havray, and Crussol featured the head of a dog on the family crests, and military leaders of France had dogs on their Blazons to symbolize vigilance and courage. The Greyhound adorned the coats of arms of more than 400 noble families in nineteenth-century France and has been the animal of honor for England's House of York since 1313.

Dog images also embellish seals and medals. Old European medallions and coins showed hunters accompanied by dogs. In Spain, the two smallest bronze coins were called *la perra chica* or "little dog" and *la perra gorda* or "fat dog."

(Above) *Frangas non flectes*—"You may break me, but you shall not bend me." Arms of Leveson-Gower, Earl Granville

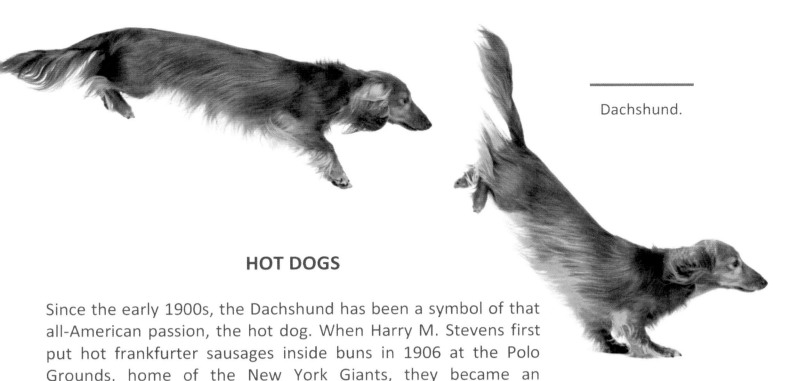

Dachshund.

HOT DOGS

Since the early 1900s, the Dachshund has been a symbol of that all-American passion, the hot dog. When Harry M. Stevens first put hot frankfurter sausages inside buns in 1906 at the Polo Grounds, home of the New York Giants, they became an immediate success.

A sports cartoonist, T.A. "Tad" Dorgan, lampooned the popular food with a cartoon Dachshund inside the bun. Dorgan coined the term "hot dog"; after all, both Dachshunds and frankfurters were red, long, and German.

Stevens embraced "hot dog" as an advertising tool, but the term backfired when people got the idea that dog meat was in the food (it wasn't). Nevertheless, the local Chamber of Commerce banned the term "hot dog" from advertising. But nobody could bury such a good name forever and today the "wiener dog" and the "hot dog" are as popular as ever.

"L'ordre du chien" (Order of the Dog) was a band of medieval knights who wore collars in the shape of a stag's head with a dog medallion that bore the motto *Vigiles* (vigilance). The order is thought to have been organized by Bouchard IV of Montmorency c. 1120.

THE DOG IN MYTH AND SUPERSTITION

The night wind whips through the trees, bringing with it the eerie bell tones of a baying hound. Soon, an echoing howl answers the lonely serenade, and then another, and another still join the chorus, until the macabre ensemble swells in awful, chilling harmony. Human hearts quicken and eyes cast about fearfully, until with chagrin they meet the curious, glistening gaze of the family dog stirring by the hearth. It has ever been so. Although a close friend to us, the dog nevertheless reminds us of all that we fear and cannot know.

Some very early religions worshipped both the wolf and the dog, which have appeared in creation fables or as fantastical creatures with supernatural powers. In South America, early people believed that human life was first released from the underworld by a dog scratching up at the earth from below.

Religions of several ancient cultures held that the passage between this world and the next was guarded by a huge dog. The Icelandic goddess of the dead is Garm, the Dog of Hel; anyone who fed the needy while on earth will find bread in their hand with which to bribe Garm for safe passage. The sacred book of the Persians (the *Avesta*) tells of a rainbow bridge guarded by a yellow-eared dog whose bark drives out the fiend from the souls of the good.

The dog has also acted as a spiritual guide. At one time in Greenland, children who died were buried with the head of a dog—a trustworthy guide into the next world. To the early people of Mexico, the dog was the symbol of the "fire from heaven" (lightning) that upon striking the ground opens the way to hell; a pet dog was killed when its owner died, and its body was placed beside the body of its master so that the dead person could safely reach the other side.

Dogs have played a role in medicine as well. Early Spaniards believed a broth of dog kidney brought relief to one suffering a bloody flux but eating the flesh of a bitch in heat could cause death. In Jamaica, hairless

---

Vulcan, the Roman god of fire and metal, forged a bronze dog that slowly came to life under his divine breath. From this dog was born Cerberus, the watchdog of Hades. Cerberus lay chained to the gates of Hades, where he fawned on those who entered and devoured those who tried to escape. Cerberus had three heads; lion, wolf, and dog, with a mane of writhing snakes, a dragon's tail, and a Mastiff's body. The ancient Romans placed a cake in the hands of their dead to pacify Cerberus. (Above) The hero Hercules wrestles Cerberus.

dogs called "fever dogs" were placed across the bodies of sick people to take away fever.

Dogs often suffered because of the superstitions associated with them. The ancient Chinese believed that demons feared black dogs; consequently, many black dogs were sacrificed so that their blood could be sprinkled to exorcise demons. During the Middle Ages in Europe, a similar belief fostered the practice of smearing the blood of black dogs on the walls of the home to protect the householder from demonic possession. In Brittany, elaborate rites supposedly forced wicked souls into black dogs, which were then ceremoniously destroyed.

During the Salem witch trials in Massachusetts (1692-1693), one of the self-confessed witches claimed the Devil appeared to her in the shape of a brown dog and a spotted female dog. Scottish folk tales mention witches worshipping a small black dog sitting on a rock. Freemasons were believed to have sold their souls to the Devil, who appeared to them in the form of a black Poodle.

But the dog has also been considered a lucky mascot. One superstition holds that if a black dog follows you home, good luck is sure to come after. Another says that to dream of a black dog or to see the likeness of a dog in the fire are both signs that a friend is near.

It is said that dreaming of dogs may indicate any number of things. Dreaming of traveling alone with a dog following you signifies steadfast friends and successful undertakings; dreaming of a friendly white dog is an omen of early marriage for a woman; and a dream of swimming dogs predicts happiness and fortune. To dream that a dog snuggles up to you indicates great gain and constant friendships, and a dream of owning a fine dog indicates future wealth.

But to dream that a Bloodhound is tracking you portends a future temptation that may mean your

To hear barking dogs predicts depressing news. Dogs growling and fighting portends one will be overcome by enemies. The baying of a dog foretells a death.

Hindu folklore holds that a dog walking between pupil and teacher nullifies the day's lessons.

downfall. A dream of vicious dogs denotes enemies and perpetual bad luck, and a dog biting you in your dreams prophesizes a disagreeable companion, either in business or marriage.

South American lore tells of dog-demons that sit in judgment of human souls. Tezcatlipoca is the Aztec Prince of the underworld in the Mexican *Book of the Dead*. He has powers over both life and death, is a bringer of disease and pestilence, and often appears as a dog or coyote. Zotz is a huge winged creature with the head of a dog that lives in the darkest regions of caves, according to ancient Mayan scriptures. Condemned souls must travel through the House of Bats, so that Zotz may receive his daily allotment of blood.

Kludde is an evil Belgian goblin, well known in Brabant and Flanders. By some he is known as Waternix, while in the countryside he is feared as a werewolf. Kludde has the power to take the form of any animal he chooses, but most often appears as a large winged black dog that walks on his hind legs. He plays brutal tricks on people, usually around twilight, knocking them down and then disappearing. One can hear the chain about his neck clanking and can recognize him by the two small blue flames that hover about his head.

Even the fictional Sherlock Holmes had a run-in with a spectral canine, in the famous tale *The Hound of the Baskervilles*; the story hinged upon the legend of the giant hound that always appeared before the death of a member of the Baskerville family.

Fiction may have its basis in fact. Even those unaware of such curses have experienced them. The fierce "Black Dog of Leeds" dates from the fifteenth century and is considered a portent of doom. This dog is thought to be the ghost of Henry VI's aunt, who was imprisoned in the castle for practicing witchcraft. The infamous Newgate Prison was said to have its own ghostly white dog that appeared at the gates before every execution.

Shawnee Legend: Our Grandmother and her dog live close to the Land of the Dead, where she weaves a basket. When the basket is finished, the world will end; but each night while Our Grandmother sleeps, her little dog unravels the day's work and buys us a little more time.

Ghost Dogs

Not all visitations of ghostly dogs are of a sinister nature. Whenever a beloved pet dies, it's natural to mourn. Some dogs are said to be reluctant to be separated from their people, even by death. Stories abound of ghostly barking and whining, spectral paws treading old, familiar paths, and phantom images lingering near loved ones.

Albert Payson Terhune, renowned writer of dog stories, had a favorite mixed-breed dog named Rex. A big, tan, short-haired dog, Rex had a distinctive scar on his face. He always stared in through the window when the Terhune family sat down to dinner.

A short time after Rex died in 1916, the Reverend Appleton Grannis, an old friend of the family, came to visit. The Reverend hadn't seen the Terhunes in years and had never met Rex. Nevertheless, while in the dining room, Grannis suddenly exclaimed to Terhune that a strange dog stared in the window at them. The dog disappeared before Terhune could turn around and see him, but Grannis described Rex perfectly, right down to the distinguishing scar on the dog's face. Two years later, another Terhune family friend swore he saw Rex lying at his feet when he visited the farm.

Are the ghosts of departed canines merely figments of human imagination? Other dogs apparently don't think so. Terhune noted that for years one of his other dogs refused to walk over ground that had been one of Rex's favorite spots.

Pierre van Paasen, a Dutch writer, tells of a black ghost dog that lived in his house and often appeared to walk past him on the stairs. One day Paasen brought two live dogs into the house. On this occasion, he did not see the ghost dog himself, but heard and watched a horrendous fight between the two live dogs and the specter. The ghost dog won.

Such ghost dogs occasionally intervene in the life of the living to good effect. Leeds Castle, a medieval fortress in the Kentish countryside near Maidstone, England, has at least three ghost dogs, and one saved a life. A visitor perched in a bay-window seat in a room located high over the moat saw a black dog walking across the room. She thought it a real dog until it disappeared into the wall. Surprised, the woman rose from her seat to investigate; abruptly, the bay window cracked and fell apart, dropping into the water below with a crash. Had she not risen to follow the mysterious ghost-dog, the woman would have plunged to her death.

The silvery gray coat, light-color eyes, and stealthy hunting prowess earn the Weimaraner the nickname "ghost dog."

Psychic Dogs

Is your dog psychic? Does he or she read your mind? When you decide to go for a walk, does Princess race excitedly to your side even before you've left your chair? Does Pepper send messages to you when he stares deeply, expectantly, into your eyes, until you somehow know his ball has fallen behind furniture beyond doggy reach?

Dr. Aristide Esser, psychiatrist and neurologist, said, "There is no doubt in my mind that some dogs, particularly those with a close relationship with their owners, have highly developed ESP." Esser conducted experiments in 1975 at Rockland State Hospital in New York, using copper-lined chambers that were sound- and vibration-proof located in different areas of the hospital. The human stayed in one chamber, his or her canine in the other. When one man acted out shooting game, his Beagles in the distant chamber went crazy, barking and whining with excitement as if experiencing a real hunting trip. In another experiment, a woman was unexpectedly confronted with an angry, threatening man; her Boxer in the other box registered a sharp increase in heart rate at the same time.

Psychic dogs seem to "know" things in advance or receive "messages" over long distances. Hunters' dogs seem able to predict whether a shot will be successful or not. Everyone who has lived with a dog has experienced this unsettling phenomenon. With a few dogs, the talent is extraordinary.

Dogs often use their abilities to save their owners' lives. In his book, *The Secret Life of Animals*, Joseph Wilder cited extraordinary examples of psychic activities in pets. A setter named Redsy one day refused to get in the boat to accompany her master on a fishing trip. The weather looked perfect, but the dog steadfastly refused to obey. Finally, the man yielded to Redsy's barked protest and canceled the day's fishing. An hour later, the great hurricane of 1938 blew in, and more than 600 human lives were lost. Did the dog detect changes in barometric pressure, or other "invisible" warnings?

Here's another example. On a camping trip, Mrs. Kearns' dog Buffy, a Keeshond, became nearly crazed when they set up camp in a small valley. Finally, Mrs. Kearns gave in to Buffy's wild insistence, and they moved the camp to a hillside. Three campers drowned that night in a flash flood after camping in the valley where Buffy had sounded her warning.

Some dogs have been able to locate people even when separated by long distances. This inexplicable talent, called "psi-trailing," has been noted for centuries, even immortalized in such classic stories as *The Incredible Journey* by Sheila Burnford and *Lassie Come-Home* by Eric Knight.

One of the best authenticated examples of canine psi-trailing is the story of Bobbie. Bobbie accompanied his family on vacation. They drove east from their home in Oregon. When they reached Wolcott, Indiana, Bobbie spied a dog fight and leaped through the car window to join the fray. By the time the car stopped, the local dogs had suspended their fight long enough to chase the intruder out of sight. A search for Bobbie proved futile. His family finally gave up, and reluctantly returned to Oregon, using a totally different route that passed through Mexico.

Six months later, an exhausted, bony, and half-starved Bobbie arrived at his home in Oregon. Affidavits by the Humane Society and others along the way proved that Bobbie didn't retrace the route through Indiana, nor did he follow the path through Mexico; Bobbie struck out straight for Oregon, traveling through the Rocky Mountains to be reunited with the family he loved.

DOG STARS

Dogs have been associated with performing probably as long as humans have sought to entertain themselves. Acrobatic dogs, juggling dogs, tightrope-walking dogs, clown dogs, football- and Frisbee-playing dogs have all amused and amazed circus-goers for centuries. With the advent of film and television, the dog got his chance to really shine.

One of the earliest canine stars was Rin Tin Tin (Rinty), a German Shepherd. Lee Duncan found Rinty as a puppy in a trench in France during World War I. Rinty became a Warner Brothers film star in the 1920s (his first film was *The Night Cry*). Fans voted this exceptional

dog the most popular film performer in 1926. When he died in 1932, his four sons carried on the tradition. Rinty number four starred in the television series *Rin Tin Tin*, and he won the 1958 and 1959 Patsy, an award given to animal actors by the American Humane Association.

German Shepherds have appeared not only in the *Rin Tin Tin* series, but also starred in *The Littlest Hobo* and *The Adventures of Champion*. The television roles of "Bullet, the Wonder Dog" on *The Roy Rogers Show*, and the bionic dog Max in *The Bionic Woman* were also played by German Shepherds.

WARNER BROS.

PRESENT

RIN·TIN·TIN

THE WONDER DOG
IN

"A HERO OF THE BIG SNOWS"

WITH
Alice Calhoun

DIRECTED BY HERMAN RAYMAKER

STORY AND SCENARIO BY
EWART ADAMSON

OTIS
LITHOGRAPH CO.

Collie popularity surged with the debut of another great canine star. Pal belonged to trainer Rudd Weatherwax. Pal play the role of "Lassie" and starred in the movie *Lassie Come-Home* in 1943. Pal lived to be nineteen years old, and Pal Jr. played Lassie on the television show. All "Lassies" have been male Collies. Lassie won so many Patsy awards that the dog was finally barred from competing.

In 1958, a dog named Spike won the Patsy for his title role in *Old Yeller*. Spike also played the dog that accompanied *The Westerner*. When the Dashiell Hammett novel *The Thin Man* became a movie series, a Wire Fox Terrier named Skippy played the part of "Asta." In 1961, Tramp, the Old English Sheepdog on the television show *My Three Sons* won the Patsy. A Great Dane named Duke brought his breed recognition when he played the title role in *The Ugly Dachshund*.

Beasley, a Dogue De Bordeaux, won the role of "Hooch" in the 1989 Tom Hanks movie, *Turner And Hooch*. Chris, the Saint Bernard, played the title role in the 1992 *Beethoven* film. The 2006 movie *Eight Below* based on a true story featured a dogsled team of eight Huskies. Other canine films include *Marley And Me*, based on the bestselling book, and Parker, a two-year-old Golden Retriever, played Enzo in *The Art of Racing In The Rain*.

Dogs don't need a pedigree to make it in the movies. Regular mutts have often stolen the show. It matters little if your dog has a pedigree or incorporates numerous breeds in his ancestry. Whether Fluffy has mastered 100 tricks or none at all we each know our dog is as gifted and handsome as any of the celebrated canines before the camera.

(Above-Left): The 1957 Lassie cast; George Chandler, Jon Shepodd, Cloris Leachman and Jon Provost. (Above-Right) Publicity picture from *The Thin Man* movie, with Myrna Loy, William Powell, and Skippy (as "Asta").

Saluki

BEST FRIENDS

Historically, the dog's most important role was as worker—hunter, shepherd, protector, and draft animal. Today, most dogs no longer perform the tasks for which they were originally bred; the dog is primarily a companion. But this is not necessarily canine choice; many dogs still yearn for the rewards of challenging work and are much healthier both physically and emotionally when given a job, even if only to fetch the morning paper. Many dogs are so much more than "just a pretty face."

A-Hunting We Will Go

Spaniels, hounds, terriers, pointers, and retrievers were all bred with a yen for the smells of the hunt, the thrill and joy of pursuit, and the pride of retrieval. Hunting dogs have been loved and celebrated in story and fable.

One of the oldest hunting breeds, the Greyhound, found a new sport at the beginning of the twentieth century. An engineer named Owen Smith came up with the idea of Greyhound stadium racing. For a time, the

Greyhound was almost exclusively a race dog, running an incredible 40 to 45 miles (64-72km) per hour. However, less than ideal care of many race dogs, especially the so-called failed racers, tarnished the reputation of the sport. Today, the breed (including retired racers), instead excel as beloved companions and couch buddies.

Lure coursing simulates hunting for live game. Sighthound breeds such as the Afghan Hound, the Whippet, Borzoi, Greyhound, Saluki, and others run in open fields in trios or pairs. Dogs work in teams to catch the plastic lure, a substitute for live prey. Dog speed, enthusiasm, follow, endurance, and agility are tested in these exciting contests.

Terriers are another old hunting breed rarely used for that purpose today. The American Working Terrier Association developed a safe Den Trial program to test the terriers' earth dog working instincts. Trials utilize buried wood-lined boxes to form nine-inch-wide

In 1878, Charles Burden's Foxhound, Old Drum, was thought by many to be the best hunting dog in America. When Burden's neighbor lost several sheep to pillaging animals, he swore to kill the next dog seen on his land. Burden was devastated when he found Old Drum shot dead. Although he couldn't prove it, he was certain the neighbor shot his dog, and filed suit for the maximum damages allowed—$50. Burden lost and appealed the case again and again until it finally reached the Missouri Supreme Court. There, he managed to obtain the service of attorney George Graham Vest, whose spontaneous oration "Tribute to a Dog" shamed the court and jury into awarding Burden compensation. From this famous speech came the saying, "The dog is man's best friend." Eighty years later, a statue in memory of Old Drum was placed on the Johnson County Courthouse lawn.

Terriers come in all shapes and sizes.

tunnels. Live rats in protective cages at the end of the boxes supply the scent and bait to induce the dogs to "hunt." The experienced tame rats are totally unconcerned; they know there's no danger. The dogs work against the clock and must run into the tunnel and show gameness in obtaining the "prey."

Barn Hunts are a relatively new sport. Any dog able to navigate through eighteen-inch-wide passages can compete. Rats are safely confined in aerated tubes hidden within a maze of hay or straw bales in this Barn Hunt Association sport.

The "Spit Dog" used in England in the 1400s helped cook meat. A rope-and-pulley mechanism led from the roasting spit to a drum-shaped wooden dog cage mounted on the wall. These dogs, usually hyperactive terriers, were locked in the cage and made to run. Think of this as a dog on a hamster-wheel. The revolving cage cranked the spit so the meat roasted evenly.

Shepherds and Sheepdogs

From the hardy, diminutive Shetland Sheepdog and Welsh Corgi to the muscular Briard, shepherd dogs share an inbred need to herd and protect. Their talent for moving seas of animals by cajoling and intimidation is impressive. Shepherds also must be fierce enough to face down foxes, wolves, and other predators to protect their charges. The instinct is so ingrained that even dogs that have never seen a sheep, cow, or reindeer will nonetheless "ride herd" on the children or other pets in their home. Traditionally, the shepherd dog protects and the sheepdog herds. However, there are a wide range of dogs that to a large extent fit both bills.

Draft Dogs

In the past, many large dogs were used to pull loads; both the Rottweiler and the Saint Bernard were bred as draft animals. Today, Belgium, Switzerland, Holland, and some German provinces still use dogs for this purpose, but the practice is carefully regulated. The sight of "Man's Best Friend" straining and grunting with his tongue hanging out is too pathetic a sight for many countries to sanction such labor.

In the United States, carting has become more an amusing pastime than actual labor for the dog. Dogs carry backpacks for hikers, pull baby carriages, and are often seen with dogcarts in local parades. The Newfoundland Club of America and Bernese Mountain Dog Club of America both offer a Draft Dog title. Weight Pull competitions allow dogs of any size to compete in contests of strength. The American Staffordshire Terriers often excel. Dogs are judged on the percentage of body weight they can pull and compete in separate weight classes.

Sled dogs like the Malamute and Husky work in teams. These dogs must be able to travel long distances in temperatures as low as 40 degrees below zero and in gale-force winds.

Sled dogs are still important in the Far North but are also trained by enthusiasts for the pure recreation of the sport. Siberian Husky Clubs and Alaskan Malamute Clubs may sponsor sledding events. Professional mushers compete in races like the famous Iditarod.

Rowdy of Nome was a Malamute that helped open the public's eyes to the wonders of his breed. He participated in the first Byrd Antarctic expedition, a 1600-mile (2560km) trek by dogsled across unknown Antarctic territory. Rowdy became famous as the "Mayor of Dog town," and for years his portrait headed the Alaskan Malamute column in the American Kennel Club Gazette. Rowdy had the honor of unveiling the Admiral Byrd Memorial to sled dogs and lived to a venerable age of twenty.

Skijoring is a major competitive sport in northern Europe, where dogs (or horses) pull a small light sled with a skier behind. In America, skijoring is a modified sport in which one or more harnessed dogs pull a cross-country skier in a race, or for fun. Any dog breed or mix can participate, although dogs weighing over 35 pounds are recommended for safety reasons.

In 1925, twenty dog sled teams relayed in a 500-mile race to bring life-saving diphtheria serum from Anchorage to Nome, Alaska to stem the epidemic. The trek that usually took a month finished in five days, and the last leg of the sprint was led by three-year-old Balto. He's come to symbolize that heroic journey, and his statue (above) in New York's Central Park commemorates the brave men and dog teams.

Law-Enforcement Dogs

German Shepherd Dogs often serve as police dogs.

The use of police dogs in London began informally in the nineteenth century when pets accompanied officer/owners on patrol. In 1938, a training school opened in England and in 1953, the training school for the Metropolitan Police Dog Section was moved to the Dog Training Establishment in Keston, Kent County. German Shepherds and Malinois (a Belgian shepherd) are used most often for law enforcement, but Labradors, Springer Spaniels, Weimaraners, Bouvier de Flandres, Airedales, Rottweilers, and Dobermans are used as well.

Shelter rescues also find work with the police and get a second chance at life. Heartwarming stories abound of dogs destined for early death, instead "enlisting" as a K9 officer, helping the community and acting as canine ambassadors and advocates for adopting throw-away dogs.

The number of law-enforcement dogs is increasing. Keen senses of smell and hearing make dogs priceless time-savers—and increase the safety of police officers. The dog also provides a deterrent to crime. You can call back a dog if the person gives up, but you can't call back a bullet. Police dogs today may specialize as a tactical dog that tracks down and holds the offender, scenting experts for explosives or drugs, and combinations of these and other skills.

TSA employs a variety of airport service dogs. U.S. Customs and Border Patrol also employs dogs, including the Beagle Brigade. These happy dogs inspect luggage and cars entering the country, to protect America's food supply and ensure dangerous agriculture isn't imported.

Military Dogs

The military "devouring dogs" of the ancients have evolved into dogs with specialized skills similar to those of police dogs. These canines train to work in the worst conditions: they run under bullet fire, and even have been parachuted into inaccessible areas. Between 1940 and 1945, eighteen dogs were decorated by the British military. Scout dogs used in the Vietnam War no longer exist in the military, but will forever live on in the memory of the men whose lives they saved.

Edinburgh Castle Cemetery for Soldiers' Dogs is a fitting memorial to the countless canines that have followed their masters into war. Markers commemorate Gyp, Yum Yum, Scamp, Major, and others. Dogs were laid to rest there from 1742 to 1982, and no one knows for certain just how many dogs are buried in the cemetery.

Edinburgh's "Bob" was an army mascot from 1853 to 1860 and won a medal in the Crimean War. Former Scottish United Services Museum curator Major H.P.E. Pereira wrote, "He is said to have shown a complete disregard for cannonballs and even chased them. More than once he was reported to have burned his nose on a hot one he did not treat with respect!"

Often, lonely soldiers far from home adopt stray dogs. When Staff Sergeant Ed Lynde rescued a skin-and-bones puppy from an enemy bunker in Iraq during the Gulf War, everyone kept telling him there was no way for him to bring "Sergeant Sandy" back home. Lynde happily proved them wrong; he raised the necessary funds, tracked down a veterinarian 300 miles (480km) away to complete the forms, and in mid-May 1991, the five-month-old puppy arrived in Oklahoma. Sergeant Sandy stood on the front lawn of Lynde's house and barked loudly at the first tree she'd ever seen in her short, hectic life.

Military dogs have acted as watch dogs, guard dogs, patrol dogs, message dogs, mine-detecting dogs, and ambulance dogs. There are dozens of memorials and monuments in America and around the world honoring the dedication and service of war dogs and their human partners. Some of these include the War Dog Memorial (PA) honoring dogs that served in World War I to the present; the National War Dog Cemetery (Naval Base Guam) that features "Cappy" a Doberman; the Fort Benning war dog memorial at the National Infantry Museum; and Military Working Dog Teams National Monument at the Joint Base San Antonio-Lackland in Texas featuring a Doberman, German Shepherd, Golden, and Malinois with their human handler.

Not all military dogs are large. Puskos, a 15-pound Jagdterrier, works for the United States Navy uncovering illegal drugs. His small size allows him to search small areas bigger dogs can't access.

(Above) Monument honors military dogs of Kyrgyzstan.

(Right) General George Patton named his Bull Terrier "Willie" after William the Conqueror.

(Below) FDR loved his Scottie dog Fala.

Sniffers

The dog possesses an incredible sense of smell. Pigs were originally used to sniff out truffles, but dogs were considered superior because they weren't tempted to eat the delicacy once found. Even Louis XV of France enjoyed hunting truffles with his favorite dog. Dogs were also used to sniff out and retrieve wild birds' eggs.

Today dogs are trained to sniff out and detect an astounding variety of items, from termites and other pests to the hydrocarbons often used by arsonists to set fires. Some dogs have been taught to use the "sniff test" to detect cancer with amazing accuracy.

Search and Rescue Dogs

The search-and-rescue (SAR) dog has been around for centuries. In 1750, Saint Bernard dogs were used by monks as guides through the soft, treacherous snow of the Alps. Often, these noble dogs saved human lives. Both Saint Bernards and Pyrenean Mountain Dogs have historically been used to find and rescue wayward travelers caught in snowstorms or avalanches.

Today, SAR dogs find missing or even hidden people, dead or alive. These dogs are used not only for avalanche work, but also in the aftermath of earthquakes, floods, natural disasters, or terrorist bomb events. Most SAR teams are not paid for their important work; dogs and human partners are volunteers dedicated to service.

The individual dog is more important than the specific breed. The most common dogs used for SAR are German Shepherds, Golden Retrievers, Labradors, Dobermans, and mixed breeds that have inherited sporting and herding traits.

Assistance Dogs

Dogs have been of extraordinary help to people in the past, and never more so than when partnered with physically challenged individuals. Dogs joyfully become our eyes, our ears, even our legs and hands, and guide us through the perils of emotional and mental anguish; they ask only love in return.

After World War I, the German government trained dogs as guides for soldiers blinded during the war. When American

Dorothy Eustis traveled breed and train German saw such a dog and sent what she had seen to Post. A young blind Morris Frank was greatly concept and convinced such a dog for him. Switzerland in April presented with a female which he promptly and Buddy were getting the word out possibilities of guide organization opened in in 1928, and a year later

to Switzerland to Shepherd Dogs, she a letter describing The Saturday Evening American man named interested in the Mrs. Eustis to train Frank traveled to 1928, and was German Shepherd, named Buddy. Frank instrumental in about the wonderful dogs. The Seeing Eye Nashville, Tennessee, moved to New Jersey.

Guide Dogs for the was founded in 1931 by Lady Kitty Ritson, of Alsatians (German Musgrave Frankland of for the Blind. Captain to be a trainer by consulted with the Liakhoff later received British Empire for this

Blind of Great Britain Muriel Cooke and breeders and trainers Shepherds), and Mr. the National Institute Liakhoff was selected Dorothy Eustis, who budding organization. the Order of the important work.

Guide dogs virtually human companions in a be witnessed to be guide dog in Australia Beau learned the

become the eyes of partnership that must believed. The first was named Beau. meaning and locations

of many kinds of shops, so that his mistress had only to say "cake-shop," "butcher," or "post office" to be guided to the appropriate place. Guide dogs not only guide, but also protect their companions. A Labrador named Dixie twice shielded her partner Doreen Cox from pickpockets, and once stopped her from falling down an open elevator shaft. To the dog, it's all in a day's work.

In 1974, a hearing-impaired woman lost a dog that had learned to be her "ears" over the years. She asked the Minnesota Humane Society to train another dog, and the society contacted Agnes McGrath, who selected and trained the first dog to aid the hearing-impaired. Signal dogs are trained to hear and alert owners to important sounds, such as the doorbell, alarm clock, crying baby, fire alarm, siren, and the like. Each dog's training is matched to the future partner's individual needs. All dogs are trained to be persistent; a signal dog must not give up until his human partner investigates the source of the sound.

The smaller breeds are typically used as signal dogs because they alert by touch, usually jumping against or on their owner. Large dogs are certainly capable of the job, but having a Newfoundland jumping into your lap is quite a different experience than having a Chihuahua do so. Mixed breeds rescued from shelters often become wonderful service dogs.

Sadie the Collie was a stray rescued by the Hearing Ear Dog Program of West Boylston, Massachusetts. She proved her worth many times over when she saved her partner Mary Lou Steger and her children from a fire in their home. A Chihuahua-mix signal dog named Chico insisted that his hearing-impaired owner, Elizabeth Smith of Watertown, Massachusetts, leave a city bus; the roof of the bus was on fire. These dogs are carefully trained, but also must know when to break the rules. Dude, a signal dog trained by International Hearing Dogs of Colorado, was taught not to bark—but barked until help arrived when his human suffered a heart attack. Every signal dog is a hero twenty-four hours a day, 365 days a year, just by giving the precious gift of independence and peace of mind to their partners.

While teaching in Asia, Bonnie Bergin, founder of Canine Companions for Independence (CCI), noticed burros used by some people to stay independent. They otherwise might have been institutionalized due to physical problems. In 1976, she placed the first CCI-trained dog. A black Labrador named Abdul

therapeutic rehabilitation to many people who suffer from mental or emotional difficulties. Therapy dogs perform such valuable services as assisting in preschools for children with development disorders and working in nursing home programs to brighten the lives of residents.

Jack Butrick and his red Doberman, Stormy, became involved with Therapy Dogs International, located in New Jersey. Stormy was happy to perform his obedience work and clown tricks for everyone. During one nursing-home visit, an elderly man petted and talked enthusiastically to Stormy and human companions; it was the first time he had spoken in months. Although Stormy later lost his right front leg to cancer, the dog refused to cut back his work on the oncology floor at Children's Hospital in Denver. "Those little guys just loved that big brave dog," said Butrick. Stormy died nine months after his leg was amputated, but in his short six-and-a-half-year life he brought joy and laughter to ease the suffering and pain of more human friends than can be counted.

transformed Kerrie Knause's life from around-the-clock care to one of freedom.

Organizations like CCI train extraordinary dogs for service with physically challenged individuals. These dogs learn to pull wheelchairs, push elevator buttons, give checks to bank tellers, operate wheelchair lifts in vehicles, retrieve dropped items, answer the phone, and generally give support to their partners wherever needed.

CCI also trains social or therapy dogs for work known as Pet-Facilitated Therapy. Therapy dogs became popular in the 1980s, when it was discovered that people who keep dogs live longer than those who don't; the calming influence of a pet reduces blood pressure and may help many health problems. Furthermore, dogs seem able to touch emotionally disturbed individuals on a level not otherwise possible.

Therapy dogs are chosen for their even temperament and affectionate nature, and bring joy, comfort, and

Assistance dogs that perform duties with a wag of the tail on a daily basis are miracles to their handlers. These dogs are more than pets; they make independence and a normal life possible. Assistance dogs combine the dogs' willing devotion with the determination of the human spirit, and together they create magic.

Assistance Dogs are not for everyone; applicants for the dogs are rigorously screened. Not every dog chosen for training works out, either; however, such dogs are usually easily placed in homes because their training makes them ideal pets. Dogs that reach retirement age (which varies according to program and individual dog) are either allowed to continue to live with their partners or are found retirement homes.

See AssistanceDogsInternational.org which provides a list of many umbrella organizations on their resources page. Contact health services organizations or humane associations for information on training centers in your area.

No longer considered gods, as in this Egyptian portrayal of Anubis (opposite page), today we often consider dogs to be gift from God, and pamper them appropriately.

Small dogs are ideally suited as signal/hearing alert dogs. They also often love to model the latest fashion in doggy gear.

Rottweiler

Three:
Physical Dog

THE ACTIVE DOG

The dog is built for endurance and strength. Unlike any other animal (except humans and monkeys), dogs are blessed with generous facial muscles that offer an incredible mobility of expression. Indeed, his whimsical face has long endeared the dog to humans. Dogs grin at us when pleased, and their furrowed brows display a distinctly perplexed expression.

Although the structure of all canine skeletons is identical, size and shape of individual bones varies from breed to breed. For instance, the German Shepherd's jaws are long and wolfy, but those of the Pekingese are short and wide. All dog skeletons contain about 319 individual bones.

How can a dog fold herself double to scratch that itch at the base of her tail, or sleep pretzeled into an area barely big enough to breathe? Dogs have five more vertebrae than we do; the extras are located behind the shoulder blades and add flexibility and mobility. A dog's neck contains seven cervical vertebrae, enabling her to turn nearly 180 degrees to look behind herself. Dogs have thirteen thoracic, seven lumbar, and three sacral vertebrae, with up to twenty-two additional vertebrae making up the tail.

Instead of a rigid collar bone, dogs have only a remnant of cartilage, and the shoulder blades are on their sides, which gives them a longer stride in running. All dogs are "digitigrade"; that is, they walk on their toes, which also lengthens their stride.

Bones of the Dog

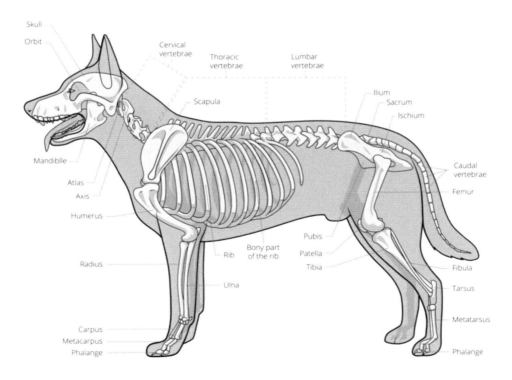

Polydactylism is the presence of extra toes, usually of the dewclaw (thumb toe) located well up the sides of the leg. Double dew claws are required in the Briard, and Great Pyrenees, but in other breeds are often surgically removed to prevent injury.

Toes and Claws

Theoretically, all dogs have five toes on each of their front feet (counting the dewclaw), and four on the hind. Each toe has a claw made of keratin that grows constantly. Claws protect the toes and are used to scratch and dig. Although they may be worn down through work or play, many must be trimmed for comfort and should clear the floor when the dog stands. Long, untrimmed nails catch in carpeting and become tangled in bedding. Often toenails curl as they grow, making it difficult for the dog to walk, and may grow into the flesh of the toe itself.

Puppies' and tiny dogs' nails may be trimmed with human nail clippers or very sharp scissors; larger dogs need heavy trimmers designed for dog nails (such as guillotine-type). Don't forget dewclaws, and never cut into the pink quick; this contains nerves and blood vessels. Cut only white or clear tips of the nails, which can be trimmed without pain, and trim no closer than 1/10 inch (25mm) to the pink portion.

Some pigmented nails hide the quick. In this case, hold trimmers so the nail is cut parallel to and only slightly shorter than the level of the toe pad; generally, the quick doesn't grow that far. If you accidentally "quick" the nail, a styptic pencil stops the bleeding. Remember, the more comfortable you make the procedure, the less trouble it will be for all concerned.

Puli

Shih Tzu

A dog's alkaline saliva contains antibacterial enzymes that help keep harmful bacteria from developing.

Fur and Shedding

Dog fur grows in cycles for short periods, rests, then dries and is shed. Length of the cycle varies with the breed, but on average it takes about 130 days to grow a coat. Changes in surrounding light trigger the shedding cycle; the more exposure to light, the more your dog will shed. House dogs exposed to long hours of artificial light seem to shed nearly year-round.

Most dogs shed at least yearly, and some twice a year. Breeds with long hair require more grooming than shorthair varieties. Curly-coated dogs like the Poodle, Komondor, and Puli (opposite page) develop corded coats when shed fur catches and remains in the coat. Shed dog hair seems magnetically attracted to our best clothes; consequently, we carry a little bit of our dogs with us wherever we go.

Cropping and Docking

In America, several breed specifications call for a docked tail and/or cropped ears. In the eighteenth century, people docked a dog's tail to prevent rabies. Also, bob-tailed dogs were considered working dogs and weren't taxed. Ears cut close to the head prevented them from being torn during work or fights.

Cropping is an expensive, painful procedure performed on nine- to twelve-week-old puppies. While under anesthesia, the dog's ear leather (pinna) is surgically cut and shaped so the ears stand erect. Ears are bandaged and stretched with splints to mold the ear to the cosmetically approved shape. Even when the wounds heal, the process of rebandaging and splinting may take up to six months, and is not always successful. Tail docking often is performed without anesthesia when puppies are three to five days old; depending on the breed, some or most of the tail is chopped off with scissors, thereby cutting off much of the canine tail semaphore communication.

Today, controversy rages over whether such cosmetic surgery is valid. Erect ears are prone to fewer infections and docked tails may prevent potential damage to working and hunting canines; however, in most cases, conformity to tradition is the true motivation for the alterations. The Council of the Royal College of Veterinary Surgeons, the Council of Europe, and the British government all oppose docking and cropping for cosmetic reasons, and it's banned in Belgium, Denmark, Finland, Germany, Great Britain, Greece, Italy, Luxembourg, The Netherlands, Norway, Portugal, Sweden, and Switzerland.

Today in America, show standards sometimes make allowances for "natural" ears and tails in some breeds. However, oftentimes show dogs have little chance of success unless they have been trimmed and docked according to accepted standards. Until breed clubs alter their standards and forbid the practice of cropping and docking, this outmoded and cruel custom will continue.

Eating and Drinking

All adult dogs have twelve incisors, four carnassials, twelve premolars, ten molars, and four canine teeth. Dogs don't chew; they only roughly chop their food, and the wide, extensible esophagus allows large portions to be swallowed. Food stays in the stomach a relatively long time. Perhaps that's why dogs like to find a good spot to sleep following every meal.

To drink, a dog curls his tongue backwards in a spoon shape, and laps very quickly to create momentum that lifts a column of water off the surface and into his mouth. Dogs swallow after every two to three laps.

The dog's sense of taste is probably as discriminating as a person's. Dogs can discern salty, bitter, acidic, and sweet tastes, and may get in trouble by overindulging a sweet tooth. In tests, smaller breed dogs show stronger and more taste preferences than larger breeds. Perhaps the stereotypical finicky toy dog isn't farfetched at all.

The dog's only sweat glands are on her feet, and function mostly as scent-marking tools rather than a cooling system. Whenever a dog feels too warm, she simply lolls her massive wet tongue out of her mouth and increases respiration. Air drawn over the tongue and passed out again takes with it moisture; panting reduces body heat by evaporation.

Touch

The dog is a social creature that thrives on touching and being touched. A dog's skin is very sensitive to both pain and pleasure. Little dogs snuggle willingly into our laps, and big dogs push as much of their heads and shoulders into our arms as possible, craving their loved one's touch.

The epidermis, the elastic dermis, and the connective tissue of the subcutis compose the three layers of skin that protect the dog from injury, infection, dehydration, and extremes of temperature. Dog skin is much thinner than human skin. Even their callused feet can be badly injured by navigating hot asphalt, grit, or stubble. Dogs are susceptible to both sunburn and frostbite, and excessive heat or cold can be fatal.

Extremely sensitive, feathery sensory nerves are dispersed beneath the skin and in the hair follicles, making each hair a responsive antenna. The most delicate touch brings a dog to attention. Outer guard hairs are exceptionally sensitive, while tactile whiskers (vibrissae) are the most sensitive of all and serve to protect the dog's face. Grazing the whiskers makes the dog flinch and blink.

The ghostly glow of canine eyes at night is caused by a layer of light-reflecting cells behind the retina. This image-intensifying mechanism, called the tapetum lucidum, acts like a mirror and reflects light back through the retina. Escaping light results in the eerie radiance.

Vision

Dogs generally have good eyesight, but it's very different from human vision. Canine eyes are situated near the front of the face, and relatively far apart, which allows for overlap that provides three-dimensional or binocular sight. The range of binocular vision varies slightly between flat-faced and narrow-headed breeds. For example, Greyhounds have about 80 degrees of canine binocular vision compared to your 120 degrees.

The colored portion of the eye, called the iris, is a muscular diaphragm that opens and closes the pupil (black portion of the eye) to control the passage of light. Both the pupil and the iris are protected by a thick, clear cornea. Behind the pupil is the lens, the focusing equipment of the eye. On the inside wall at the back of the eyeball is the "movie screen," or retina. The retina contains receptors that respond to light (rods) and color (cones).

The iris expands and contracts depending on the amount and intensity of the available light. The dog sees when light passes through the pupil and is focused by the lens onto the retina. There, rods and cones send signals through the optic nerve to the brain, which translates the data into pictures and tells the dog what he sees.

Dogs lack a fovea, a small rodless area of the retina that provides detail vision in humans. A dog may not recognize a fast-approaching object, and indeed, must back up to see anything that's too close. The dog's binocular field of vision is less than a person's, so dogs don't judge distance very well. However, many short-nosed dogs like Bulldogs have a spot on the retina (area centralis) composed of high-density vision cells, while long-nosed breeds like Greyhounds have a visual streak on the retina. The visual streak aids in long-distance vision, while the area centralis allows for better near vision.

Most dogs rely on movement to notice something in their visual range. That's why a motionless object 300 yards (270m) away is virtually invisible, but at a distance of a mile (1.6km), the dog can see and respond to strong hand signals. Dogs have more light-sensitive cells than we do, so their night vision is much better than ours.

It used to be thought that dogs only saw in shades of black and white. A large number of rods in the eyes gives dogs an advantage during the monochromatic twilight, but dogs do have cones, and therefore are able to see some degree of color. Studies have shown that dogs see reds and blues, and with more difficulty, can distinguish oranges and yellows. To dogs, color just isn't very important. Even so, it's nice to think that our dogs at least have the potential to share our human love of color.

The inner corner of the eye has a third eyelid or haw (nictitating membrane). The haw acts like a windshield wiper and can cross from the inside corner of the eye to the other side to clean, lubricate, and protect. Some dogs have an obvious haw, while it's almost invisible in others.

Sound Sense

The dog's extraordinary sense of hearing offers a valuable aid to humans. Whether floppy, erect, hairy, or bald, the dog's external ears (pinna) are very mobile and can swivel as much as 180 degrees to capture sound. The pinna collects, directs, and reflects air vibrations into the auditory canal, where they strike against the tympanic membrane, also called the ear drum. Sound waves set the membranes into sympathetic vibration, amplified by a chain of three bones, the auditory ossicles. The ossicles pass vibrations on to the cochlea, fluid-filled tubes that translate the vibration into nerve impulses. The nerve impulses are conducted by the auditory nerve to the brain, and there interpreted as sound.

Dogs hear approximately the same low pitches as we do, but their higher range is much better than ours. Human ears can perceive about 20,000 cycles per second; tests indicate that dogs hear waves of frequency as high as 100,000 per second. Dogs can invariably hear the difference between an opening cupboard door that holds doggy shampoo and one that contains puppy crunchies. Even Charlie Brown observed that Snoopy

The French Bulldog (above) is known for her expressive, large ears.

can hear the "munch" of a marshmallow— just like a real dog.

Countless songs celebrate dogs: "Old Dog Tray, " "How Much Is That Doggy In The Window," Elvis Presley's "Old Shep" and "You Ain't Nothin' But A Hound Dog" were all howling successes.

Some dogs are musicians in their own right; the barking rendition of "Jingle Bells" never fails to make holiday shoppers cringe. The Paul Winter Consort's haunting duet of wolf howls and a saxophone is truly inspirational.

Do dogs appreciate music? Exceptional hearing certainly gives them the potential. Lady, parents' Sheltie, loved music, and invariably curled up beneath the piano whenever someone played, risking her nose each time the pedal was pressed. Later, her Sheltie successor, Pickles, enjoyed piano just as much, and liked singing as long as the range was moderate. Pickles telegraphed her opinions by tipping her nose to the ceiling and howling distaste. Everyone's a critic.

Scent Sense

Humans take scent for granted. We enjoy the fragrance of cologne and relish the smell of a barbecue, grimace with distaste at the scent of a skunk, and choke on smoky car exhaust. Humans deodorize garbage cans, sprinkle carpet powders, and use scented vacuum bags; we buy perfumed cleaners and "all natural" sprays for scenting our homes, ourselves, and even our pets. If a smell isn't pleasant, we cover it up.

Dogs, on the other hand, were born to smell and be smelled. Dogs depend on their awesome olfactory ability for identification, social interaction, and communication. Scent is more important than vision or hearing.

The dog's olfactory sense aids people to find everything from edible fungi, such as truffles, to explosives, drugs, and escaped convicts. All dogs can smell a single drop of blood mixed in five quarts (4.7l) of water, and some specialist scenting dogs are even more adept. Bloodhounds can track a four-day-old trail for up to 100 miles (160km).

The dog's normally cool, moist nose helps retain and assimilate scent chemicals riding on the air. The nose includes the external nares (nostrils) and a nasal cavity divided by a partition into two passages (one for each nostril) that run the entire length of the muzzle. The partition is formed from a massive scroll-bone encased within thick, spongy mucous membranes rich in blood vessels, ethmoidal scent cells, and nerve endings. The nerve endings transmit the most minute olfactory impression directly to the brain.

Items that smell like YOU prove irresistible to dogs like this German Shorthair Pointer puppy.

In humans, the actual scent mechanism contains five to twenty-million scent cells. In the dog (a German Shepherd, for instance), there are about 200 million ethmoidal cells. Smaller dogs have fewer scent cells than larger dogs, but even so, a Dachshund has 125 million such cells.

A dog's nose print is as distinctive and individual as a human fingerprint.

The dog's scenting ability depends on what he smells. Some smells probably don't mean anything to the dog, but for certain chemicals the dog's ability is phenomenal. The dog's sense of smell is at least a million times better than a person. To the dog, sniffing is the next best thing to heaven.

Dogs have a second scent-detecting organ called the vomeronasal organ (Jacobson's organ) in the roof of the mouth behind the front teeth. Pheromones (scent chemicals unique to dogs) are transferred to the organ when the dog touches his tongue to the roof of his mouth after licking to pick up a scent. A dog will typically puff out his cheeks or chatter his teeth to read the pheromone messages left by another dog.

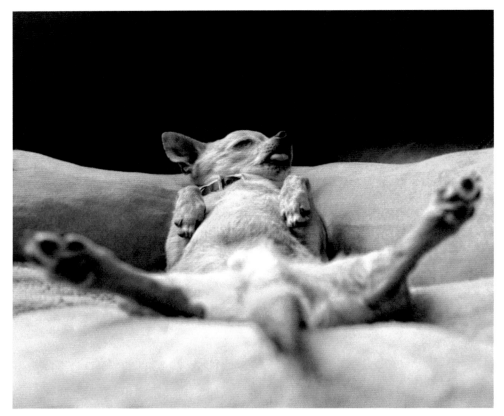

DOG BEHAVIOR

Dogs are extremely intelligent; in fact, they're so smart they often train their owners instead of the other way around. You provide for and protect your dog, but that's not enough to keep him healthy and happy. Dogs are social creatures that need structure and guidance. Some dogs naturally challenge us, so a position of authority must be established early and routinely reinforced. By all means, be your dog's friend; but be sure you are also the one in charge in your family.

Rules of the House

Numerous excellent references provide guidance for training your dog (see page 153), but there are different schools of thought as to what method works best. Some basic guidelines remain universal.

All puppies should learn the meaning of a solid, authoritative "No!" This is often all that's necessary to correct poor behavior. Also remember that fear and pain interfere with and block learning and have no place in training. Period.

Talk to your dog. Dogs learn a huge vocabulary, and the more a puppy understands, the fewer behavioral problems there will be.

Dogs are very sensitive to nuances of sound and facial expressions, and often react more to emotion and body language than specific words. Be sure your vocal tone and expression reflect what you mean; shaming your pet while you laugh is pointless, and sending mixed signals only confuses the animal.

Learning should be an enjoyable process for you both. Most dogs idolize their human and want to please you but dwelling on negatives will teach your dog he gets more attention for doing something wrong. Remember, too, that discouragement can make the dog give up. Always end a session on an up note—pick something you know your dog can do. Then reward successful behavior with something he loves.

If your dog doesn't understand your instruction, it's not fair and can even be detrimental to reprimand. Praise enthusiastically when your pet does something right—when she comes on command or chews the rawhide toy instead of your high heels. Consistency is key. Do your best to catch your dog in the act—of doing something RIGHT, and then praise and reward her. She'll be excited and eager to find new ways to please you and make you both happy.

When your dog refuses to follow a command, rather than punish, simply offer no reward. Any attention, even shouting, may be perceived as a reward. Ignoring the bad behaviors, and rewarding good choices works wonders especially with puppies.

Growling upsets people, but shouldn't be quashed, because it's a warning to you born from fear, discomfort, or defense. You WANT your dog to let you know when he's upset and tell you what causes him to growl. Then you can address the trigger(s) that cause the growling. Quashing the growl may prompt dogs to go directly to a bite without the warning!

Be aware that some dogs, (especially certain breeds) growl to "talk" to us, and the growly-grumble sound in these instances may be signs of happiness. A growly dog may require help from a qualified behavior or training professional to understand what's going on, and determine what, if anything, should be done.

Effective Correction & Rewards

Use reprimands only during or immediately following poor behavior. Dogs have short memories when it comes to infractions and punishing after the fact won't correct the behavior; no dog understands the shoe chewed three hours ago has anything to do with the here and now. Chasing after the dog as you scold will either make him fear you or believe you're playing a game.

Firm verbal correction (never shout) is effective alone or in combination with other forms of reprimand. With very sensitive dogs, a disappointed "Shame on you!" may suffice. Abrupt noises startle and interrupt poor behavior. A coffee can filled with loose change rattled loudly at appropriate times, along with a verbal reprimand, often works wonders. Corporeal punishment is ineffective and often damages the dog's personality. Never slap or hit your dog; he will learn to associate your hands with punishment.

Clicker training works exceedingly well. The clicker marks the behavior you like (when he SITS), and a tiny treat along with praise rewards the dog. Food rewards bring fast results, and later are offered only intermittently to encourage dogs to perform anytime—not just when they see a treat. Most dogs react very well to verbal praise alone, or even rewarding with a favorite toy or game (Frisbee anyone?). Please consider obedience training for your dog. Your veterinarian's office or pet products store may be able to recommend trainers in your area. Hint: it works better if you train with your dog!

Treat rewards work best if they're something dogs don't get any other time. Tiny amounts are best, so they don't disrupt his appetite. BEWARE OF TOXIC TREATS: Chocolate contains dangerous theobromine, and grapes are deadly for dogs.

Dinner Time!

Today you have a plethora of dog foods from which to choose. Your veterinarian or breeder often shares great advice on the best product for your individual canine. Commercial foods are convenient, and offer specific diets designed for the growing puppy, the healthy adult, geriatric senior dogs, and even canines with specific health concerns. Very generally, puppies should be fed three times a day until at least six months of age, and twice daily thereafter. Some dogs do well on once daily meals. It's also possible to provide home prepared food for your dog. Your veterinarian can recommend a good brand of food, the proper feeding schedule, and the right amount for your pet's size, age, and energy needs.

Feed at the same time and place each day. Usually, fifteen minutes offers enough time to eat, after which pick up the food. That teaches your dog to eat at mealtime, and not hold out for something better, like the leftovers from your plate. Some people food may be fine, but too many rich fatty scraps aren't healthy and can upset a dog's digestion. Dogs evolved as gorgers, and if they eat a lot one day, they may skip the next meal with no ill effect. Soon your dog will learn to eat what is offered before it is removed—and you'll be able to tell when he might really be ill as opposed to goldbricking for handouts

Puppies often indulge in coprophagia, a nasty, yet quite common habit of eating animal droppings. Mother dogs clean up after puppies, so the copycat behavior often arises in youngsters. Most dogs outgrow the behavior. Your veterinarian can recommend products that give feces a bad taste to deter the habit.

Mounting Inappropriately

In an unaltered male dog, a level of sexual frustration can build until he attempts to mate with anything that doesn't move: the table, a chair, your leg. Dogs think that humans are members of the same species and grab legs because they are easy to clasp. Neutering relieves you both of the physical and emotional turmoil. However, some neutered dogs continue the habit.

In most mammals, adult males have a higher level of testosterone than youngsters. But in dogs, the testosterone levels rise at four to five months of age, and by age ten months, juvenile testosterone levels can be up to five times greater than that of an adult male dog. The corresponding scent allows adult dogs to recognize adolescent pups and teach them to respect their elders.

Jumping on People

A small dog jumping up on people may be cute or simply annoying, but large dogs can cause injury. Be consistent; your dog won't understand why it's okay to jump on you, but not on Grandma. Pushing a playful dog away (even with your knee) invites further play and greatly excites the dog. Stepping on the dog's toes associates pain with an affectionate bid for attention.

Dogs jump up to reach and lick your face, a canine signal of deference. So yelling or shaming typically makes the behavior worse when he makes even greater effort to lick your face to diffuse your angst. Instead, turn your back on the jumping dog (he wants face-to-face interaction), and teach him instead to SIT for attention. Once he plants his tail, reward him with attention for his polite behavior.

Let dogs delight to bark and bite,
For God hath made them so...
Isaac Watts (1674-1748)

Do you REALLY want to reward jumping up? Think about your own behavior, too.

Digging

Many dogs, particularly terriers, enjoy digging. Provide the excavator with a legal digging place where he can tunnel to his heart's content. Fence off-limits areas or supervise constantly and prevent inappropriate digging. Areas that you want to protect can be booby-trapped with the dogs buried feces as a most effective deterrent.

Do You Speak Dog?

Dog dialogue isn't easy to master. Dog communication uses sounds, body signals and smells. We aren't equipped to interpret the finer points, but most dog lovers understand more than they think.

A dog's direct stare and snarl warn you to keep your distance. Running from a dog or making any quick motions stimulates a dog's chase and attack instincts. When threatened by a strange dog, hold your ground, avert your eyes, or back up very slowly with a smooth motion.

Aggression within limits is natural. Posturing prevents actual fights and gives dogs the opportunity to diffuse stressful situations. Threatening dogs typically fix opponents with intimidating stares, snarl to reveal teeth, and hold their ears erect. With arched neck and high-held head, movement is stiff, and fur along the back stands on end. Threatening dogs may lift a leg and urinate, then scratch the ground while bristling and growling.

Usually such a display prompts one dog to back down; however, some encounters escalate to attack. An attacking dog plasters his ears against the side of his head, probably to protect them. During intense threat or attack, the head lowers and neck extends as the dog "points" his adversary.

Submissive body language is the reverse of aggressive displays. Aggressive dogs try to look bigger by fluffing out their fur and standing on their toes; the submissive pooch wants to appear smaller. Just as aggressive displays encourage distance, deference displays invite proximity.

Adult dogs have strong inhibitions about attacking puppies; therefore, subordinate adult dogs act like puppies to avoid being attacked. When threatened, a dog shows "no threat" by crouching, rolling onto his back to expose the genitals, and perhaps even urinating in the ultimate deference display. To approach a dominant figure, the dog crouches to appear "puppy-size," then crawls forward and reaches up to lick and nuzzle the face the same way puppies beg food from adults or attention from humans.

Some dogs urinate when verbally corrected, and others urinate from excitement when you come home. Punishing submissive urination makes it worse, because the dog figures he must be even more submissive and so increases the waterworks. Most puppies outgrow it. Adult dogs that persist in submissive urination often learn to control themselves if you ignore them the first five to ten minutes after returning home.

Other signs of deference include avoiding eye contact in an exaggerated fashion; ears flattening against the head; tucking the tail or wagging in a low position; tongue flicking out to indicate a desire to lick; and raising or offering a forepaw, a prologue to rolling over. These behaviors also serve to diffuse potential aggression from other dogs, and sometimes are called "calming signals." Ambivalent signals occur when a dog feels conflicting emotion. Maybe she's fearfully aggressive, or curious but worried at the same time. The fear-biter may show elements of aggression along with fear; hackles may be raised, but tail tucked tight, with an aggressive facial expression.

The fearless dog attacks in silence. A snarl indicates slight fear. Growling shows deeper fear, and barks changing to or mixed with growls indicate the dog is probably more fearful than aggressive. The timid dog flees in silence.

Woofs, Snarls, Howls & Whimpers

The phonation that produces the dog's voice varies depending on size and shape of vocal cords and muzzle, as well as speed and power of lung capacity. The dogs' vocal repertory is tied to body movement and generally indicates emotional state.

Whining is a distress call aimed at humans; the pleading sound often occurs when a dog is left alone, feels frustrated, or is punished. The bark serves as a canine alert that warns the family of anything unusual, like the arrival of a friend or stranger, and is not necessarily a sign of aggression.

Howls basically mean, "I am here; please join me," and in wolves and other wild canids, establishes territory and calls the pack together. If isolated, some dogs howl from loneliness. In musical families, the singing or playing of instruments often prompts dogs to join in what they perceive to be a friendly howl-along.

Excessive barking aggravates humans and can be a sign of boredom. Breeds with a watchdog background may be more prone to overindulge. Allow and even praise initial barking; the dog has alerted the family (you), so acknowledge a job well done. Continued barking should be halted with an appropriate command, such as "Enough," or "Quiet." Don't yell; yelling may be perceived as a "barking contest," and your dog will happily join the competition.

Tail of the Dog

To humans, a wagging tail conveys joy, but tail wagging has multiple meanings depending on what the rest of the dog's body says. Basically, the tail is held high by confident dogs, and low or tucked by shy or insecure canines. In submissive dogs, wags are loose and wide, while aggressive dogs wag in short arcs and may wag to signal imminent attack. The highly held tail allows anal sniffing and scent identification; the tucked tail cuts off this avenue of exploration, just like a shy human hiding the face.

Sniffing

When dogs meet, they first smell each other's faces, then direct their attention to each other's anal area. Wagging with the tail held high spreads the anal gland scent on the air. Anal glands are two pea-size organs located on each side of the rectum that add a strong-smelling scent to feces and give each dog an individual scent identity. Dragging the rump, or scooting, is usually a means of seeking relief from impacted anal glands, which occur more commonly in small dogs.

Leg Lifting & Rolling

At puberty, a male dog starts marking behavior. He cocks his leg against different objects to spray urine. What do the scent marks mean? Dog urine contains sexual information, allows individual identification, and may indicate "occupied" territory. Leg-cocking enables the scent to be placed at doggy nose level; an upright object (such as a fire hydrant) may act as a visual signpost, telling other dogs where to sniff. Dogs become enraptured reading the scented Post-It notes left by others, then obliterate the marks with their own.

In laboratory settings, dogs go into a kind of "scent ecstasy" and roll on almost any strong odor, including lemon rind, tobacco, and perfume. Frequently, dogs roll in more noxious aromas—the equivalent of dabbing on doggy perfume. To your dog, rotten fish or ripe cow pats may be the essence of high fashion. Some behaviorists theorize rolling allows them to carry interesting smelly information back home to share with other dogs—or their human companions. People rarely appreciate the gesture.

REPRODUCTION

Dogs can sire puppies by ten months, and some bitches experience their first heat (estrus) as early as six months. Estrus usually occurs about every six to eight months and lasts twenty-one days.

Proestrus, the onset of the heat cycle, lasts six to nine days. You'll notice a dark bloody discharge and swelling of the vulva. Standing heat, the receptive phase when the bitch accepts the male's advances, occurs during ovulation, and the discharge lightens from dark red to a faint pinkish color. Standing heat lasts about six to twelve days and ends when the bitch refuses the male. Dogs breed between day ten and day fourteen of estrus.

During ovulation, eggs that are shed must mature for seventy-two hours before they can be fertilized by sperm; however, the dog's sperm is able to survive up to seven days in the uterus.

In arranged breedings, the bitch is sent to the male dog. He makes his own explorations, sniffing and posturing, while the female acts coy and flirtatious; she'll flag and raise her tail to the side, and present her vulva to him when she's ready. The stud dog mounts the female, clasps her with his forelegs, and inserts his penis. At full penetration, he stops thrusting forward, and treads up and down with his hind paws.

When a knot at the base of the penis (bulbus glandis) becomes swollen, it's held firmly by the muscles of the vagina, causing the mating dogs to become "tied" together. The swelling induces ejaculation, which occurs in three stages; an initial clear sperm-less fluid is followed by a second ejaculation containing sperm, and then a final third ejaculation of prostatic fluid propels the sperm into the uterus. The prolonged tie seems to be a way of ensuring enough time for the process to be complete. The tie lasts three to forty minutes and sometimes longer; duration has no effect on success of mating or the number of resulting puppies.

Gestation is usually about sixty-three days. A veterinarian can determine pregnancy by palpation at about twenty-six days of gestation, but later than that the uterus becomes filled with fluid and the "puppy bumps" are no longer discernible. If breeding has been successful, the first clear sign will be an enlarging and darkening of the nipples at about forty days of gestation.

A few days before the birth, the mother-to-be begins to look for a good place to bear her puppies. She may go about in a flurry of activity, rummaging in closets or rearranging her bedding. Provide her with a special,

A greyhound named Timmy of London, England, sired more than 3,024 puppies in an eight-year period.

Litter size varies depending on breed, but the average is five puppies. An American Foxhound named Lena bore a record litter of twenty-three puppies in 1945.

private place to give birth. This may prevent her from whelping on your bedspread. She should already be sleeping in the whelping box by the time her puppies arrive.

Eight to twelve hours before whelping, the expectant mom's temperature abruptly drops about two degrees (1° C). The first stage of labor begins with rapid panting, anxiousness, straining, and possibly vomiting. Each puppy is encased in a bag of fluid that helps lubricate the passage; if the bag ruptures during delivery, a straw-colored fluid will be passed, and should be shortly followed by a puppy. The placenta, or afterbirth, follows each birth. A retained placenta can cause problems, so be alert. Puppies are born fifteen minutes to two hours apart.

If a puppy feels very cold and acts weak, dunk it up to its neck in a bowl of 101°F (38°C) water (the average puppy body temperature) for two to three minutes. Then stroke and massage until it becomes more active, and dry with warm towels. If the puppy is too weak to breathe, squeeze the chest gently from side to side and back to front; mouth-to-nose respiration (very gentle breaths!) may stimulate breathing. Have a veterinarian check on the new mother and her puppies the day after delivery.

When to Get Help

During the Birth: If bearing down produces no puppies after two hours; if a dark green or bloody discharge passes before the first puppy's birth (after the first birth this discharge is normal); if clear yellow (amniotic) fluid appears and a puppy isn't delivered within thirty minutes; if the mother is in extreme pain (trembling, shivering, or collapsing); or if labor stops before all puppies are delivered.

After the Birth: If there is a heavy, dark, bloody greenish or tomato soup-like discharge accompanied by fever; if the mother acts lethargic; if normal eating doesn't resume in twelve hours; if she is abnormally restless; if she exhibits stiff-legged jerky pacing with rapid respiration; or if she shows no interest in her puppies.

PUPPY DEVELOPMENT

Dalmatians are born white. Spots develop later.

As each puppy is born, the bitch breaks the membrane and licks them to stimulate breathing and circulation. She shreds the cord, and often eats the afterbirth. Puppies immediately seek a breast; the first milk (colostrum) contains important antibodies and nutrients.

If the mother doesn't open the sack, do it yourself, and rub the baby vigorously with warm towels to stimulate breathing. Tie the cord and cut about two inches (5cm)

from the abdomen, then disinfect the cut end with iodine. Use a bulb syringe to clear fluid from the mouth; or, hold the puppy securely and fling it head-down between your legs toward the floor, so centrifugal force clears the passages.

A newborn's eyes and ears are sealed, but its sense of smell is already well developed. Puppies use their heads and faces as sensors to find warm, soft surfaces. Each puppy competes with its littermates for the best nipple.

The puppies spend about 10 percent of the time eating, and the rest sleeping together in a pile. A puppy's ability to regulate body temperature isn't well developed until two to three weeks of age. At birth, its temperature ranges from 92° to 97°F (33° to 36° C), but close body contact with its mother and siblings keeps temperature 96° to 100°F (35° to 38° C).

Puppies' eyes and ears open at ten to sixteen days. Crawling begins at birth, and wobbly standing occurs at about fifteen days. By three weeks, puppies are walking and getting into all kinds of trouble; but the baby's accompanying tail wagging and barking that begin at this age keeps you smiling through each trespass.

Twenty-eight milk teeth erupt between three and five weeks of age; large breed dogs teethe earlier than toy breeds. The mother's milk diminishes at about the same time, and she begins to wean her puppies in earnest; it generally takes a week for the puppies to get the message. At this age, puppies naturally imitate her, and will lap soft food from a bowl.

At about four to five weeks, puppies chase each other and grab the scruff of necks. They learn and perfect the prey-shaking head movements. Through pounce and snap, growl and snarl, bared fang and offered tummy, they learn to show submission, confidence, and invitation to play. By five weeks, unique facial expressions evolve as puppies learn to manipulate ears and lips, and display teeth. An extensive vocal repertoire develops; puppies become proficient at barks, snarls, yipes, and whines, each carrying important meaning.

At this age, they begin to urinate and defecate in one designated area some distance from their beds. Both male and female puppies squat to urinate; male leg-cocking begins at eight or nine months. By six weeks, the puppy has learned its lessons and knows all the behavior patterns of the adult.

Proper socialization is extremely important. Expose puppies to a variety of safe, positive situations: invite guests to handle and play with them, allow your other (healthy) dogs and cats to interact with them. Responsible breeders often crate train puppies early by letting them play and eat in the dog crate together, so the crate becomes a "happy place."

Orphan puppies must be fed three to four times daily (the amount depends on the puppy's weight), and during the first three weeks must be stimulated to eliminate. After each feeding, gently massage the anal area with cotton dipped in warm water.

Poorly socialized puppies grow fearful of strange situations and may become either extremely shy or fear biters.

Depending on the breed, your puppy won't be an adult until twelve to eighteen months of age. A one-year-old dog is physiologically equal to a thirteen-year old-child, and a two-year-old dog is like a twenty-year-old adult. From age three on, each year is equivalent to about five of ours; however, giant-breed dogs like Great Danes tend to age much more quickly than Toy breeds.

Let's Play

Aside from just plain being fun, play helps develop motor and social skills and prepares puppies for life. At the age of three weeks, puppies chew each other's ears, and lick, bite, and paw Mom's and each other's faces. This important learning experience teaches puppies just how hard they can bite (or be bitten) without causing pain. The pups soon discover how to inhibit the bite.

By five weeks, puppies often carry things around. They play tug-of-war and may even guard a toy or piece of food.

Dogs play their entire adulthood. In order to make clear that the playful chasing, fleeing, and growling is not real, dogs use elaborate meta signals to show everything that comes after is meant as a game. The most obvious invitation to play is the canine bow, when the rear end is stuck high in the air with waving tail, while the forequarters lower the chest to the ground. Dogs also display a grinning play face as well as nudge with their noses, paw, and offer an object to invite a game of keep away. Sometimes they display exaggerated jumping and twirling, running and zigzagging. Dominant dogs may offer a reassurance display; they flop on their backs and pretend to be submissive, so the other dog feels brave enough for play to begin.

The Healthy Puppy

By eight weeks of age, a puppy may leave Mom to go to a new home. The puppy will be better socialized, though, by staying with littermates and Mom until twelve weeks. Other dogs teach bite inhibition and how to get along with other dogs better than humans can.

When selecting a puppy, always choose a healthy animal; sick puppies start life with several strikes against them. The eyes and nose should be free of discharge; the nose should be cool and moist, the gums pink; the inside of ears ought to look and smell clean; the coat must be bright and shiny, and skin should be free of scabs, scales, redness, or bald spots; the anal area must be free of diarrhea or discharge; and male puppies ought to have both testicles visible. Puppies should be happy, alert, very active, and playful. Shrinking violets and aggressive cases haven't been properly socialized, and both extremes cause problems. The perfect puppy follows you with her tail held high, is active, thrives on petting, may struggle when initially held but then relaxes and accepts being picked up.

When lifting your puppy, cup her bottom with one hand and her chest (behind the forelegs) with the other. Lift adults with the same care, supporting both chest and hindquarters. Never lift a dog by the front legs.

A Gnawing Habit

To playful puppies, everything is a toy to be bitten, chewed, and shaken. Chewing also helps a puppy's adult teeth break through, which happens at above four months. In the wild, adult wolves bring prey to the den for cubs to practice killing, and it's natural for a puppy to treat anything you leave laying around as fair game.

Teething puppies are notorious chewers, and dogs enjoy chewing as adults, too. Dogs need to chew to maintain oral hygiene and chewing also has a calming effect. Repellants may protect treated objects from an ardent chewer but limiting opportunities to chew the wrong thing goes a long way toward changing problem behavior.

Avoid offering old shoes, socks, children's toys, or other hand-me-downs to your pet. He won't know the difference between an old shoe and your new loafers. When the puppy turns your personal items into playthings, immediately offer to trade with a "legal" toy—and learn to keep illegal items out of puppy reach. Ideal toys include dental chew toys, stuffed sterilized bones from pet products stores, or rawhide bones that indulge the dog's urge to chew.

Never give your dog cooked bones (they splinter) or allow sticks or rocks as chewing toys. They may damage teeth and cause deadly obstructions or punctures if swallowed.

Older dogs that chew inappropriately may be bored or lonely. Make sure lots of acceptable chew toys are available. Try to determine what's causing the chewing—is the dog alone much of the time? Does she get enough exercise? When you've identified the problem, you can try to correct it. Some dog behaviorists recommend getting your pet a pet—if not another dog, then a cat, fish, turtle, hamster, or even a parakeet to watch may divert a chewer for hours. Keep in mind the new pet will need attention from you, too!

Puppy Puddles and Plops

Dog lovers dread the unpleasant surprises that are inevitably left scattered about the house by a new puppy. Unless you plan to use paper-training for life, housetraining your puppy to use an outside area for elimination without the intermediate paper chase offers a quicker and more effective option. Crate training works great as a teaching tool.

Anticipate the dog's internal clock (after naps, meals, and playtime) and always take her to the same place so she identifies that area as the potty spot. Babies have smaller bladders, and less capacity to hold it so be sure to offer plenty of opportunities to eliminate. A two-month-old baby can wait two hours, a three-month-old pup can hold it three hours, and so on, but don't make your pup wait too long. Also, teach a "potty command" so your dog learns what you want. One we use for our dogs is *take a break* so they take care of business immediately before allowed to run around and sniff and play. When a mistake happens in the house, avoid scolding. That could teach the puppy to HIDE the deposit. Instead, if in the act, simply scoop up the puppy, and remove her to the designated area. Always praise enthusiastically whenever your puppy relieves herself in the right place.

If you find a puddle or plop after the fact, shame on YOU, because you didn't supervise appropriately. And when you cannot supervise your baby dog, confine her to the crate. This isn't cruel—make the crate a fun, happy place with special toys she only gets when in the confinement. Dogs avoid messing their bed, so confining her to a space only large enough for bedding and a small bowl of water means she'll let you know when she needs to eliminate. Even the kitchen or laundry room is a huge space to a tiny puppy, and she will simply eliminate in one corner and sleep in the other.

The alternative means living with adult-size puddles and plops, which are unthinkable, particularly if you've chosen a Malinois, like the dog pictured below. Instead of crating, you may wish to leash the puppy to your belt and constantly supervise. Discontinue crating or the leash connection only when the puppy consistently warns you of her needs. It may take longer, but many puppies learn within the first several days or a week.

Many local governments have enacted pooper-scooper laws that enforce good manners among dog owners. Generally, these laws require you to immediately and sanitarily dispose of droppings deposited anywhere except on your own property. When on your own property, sanitation dictates prompt removal as well, to help prevent spread of parasites. Diet can help reduce both the bulk and odor of solid wastes. Dogs "go" in the wrong places for any number of reasons. They may be reacting to changes in your home—a new baby, marriage, divorce, or the addition of a new pet or loss of an old pet. Insufficient training may be at fault, or the dog may use bodily functions to challenge authority and exhibit displeasure. Most importantly, dogs break training when they're sick. Whenever an accident occurs, be sure you know why, so you can act appropriately to prevent recurrence.

Once the dog starts using a corner of the room, it's a hard habit to break. Clean accidents with a commercial odor neutralizer or enzymatic cleanser to discourage a repeat performance. Adult dogs that habitually leave little presents around the house may benefit from a reminder of bathroom etiquette with a repeat of crate training. The key to a future free of annoyance is your patience today, along with consistency. Your entire family, (and your carpet) will love you for it

Belgian Shepherd (Malinois)

The Second Pet

Introduce new dogs on neutral territory like the dog park that neither pet feels the need to defend. Introductions to cats should be done through a solid door to get both pets used to the idea with preliminary sniffing.

Allow them to get acquainted first while under leash control, and if positive, allow dogs to play together. Most dogs enjoy meeting new canine friends. Have a friend bring the new pet, so you aren't blamed for the intrusion. It's natural for the old-timer to growl to teach a younger, newer dog boundaries, but excessive roughness shouldn't be tolerated. Be sure to give the older pet plenty of attention, so he doesn't feel displaced.

Nobody's Dog

Today, I found Nobody's Dog. Her ribs were beginning to show through a once shiny black coat. At first, she tucked her tail tightly and ran, then, ever hopeful, returned with a tentative wag.

I bet she was cute as a puppy. Somebody picked her out special, took her home, and made her believe she would always be loved.

But some humans change their minds and their loves as often as dirty socks. Even so, the betrayed black dog still loves them, futilely waiting for them to come back for her. She had a name once, and now she can't understand, for you see, a dog's love never dies.

Today, I found Nobody's Dog, one of millions abandoned each year by owners that take the coward's way out. They won't see her slowly starve or freeze to death, be hit by a car, or live at the mercy of strangers as she begs for a scrap of attention.

Today, the Shelter rescued Nobody's Dog. There, she'll be fed, she'll be loved, and hopefully she'll be claimed by a more fitting, deserving human. If not, she'll go to an even better place, one where dogs are always loved and are never thrown away on a cruel whim. But she still yearns to be Somebody's Dog once more.

Canine Responsibility

Every second, another puppy is born; each minute, dozens of new furry faces yipe and cry; every hour, thousands of puppies are added to the horrendous total. According to the ASPCA, 3.9 million dogs enter shelters each year, and 30 percent are euthanized. Countless more are abandoned because there just aren't enough good homes to go around.

No one can deny that a cuddly puppy is adorable, and that a basketful of the wee beasties is the ultimate in fuzzy puppy love. But it's essential that all dog lovers realize their responsibility to prevent rather than perpetuate puppy births. There is indeed a litter problem, and not just along the highways. Informed dog lovers know the "puppy-lation" explosion isn't a result of love, but of ignorance and mismanagement.

Unless you're a professional, it's a crime against dogdom to breed your dog, male or female. Each litter member that finds a home eliminates a prospective sanctuary for another puppy; in effect, producing puppies sentences others to death. There is no valid excuse to allow any dog to roam and breed indiscriminately. Spayed and neutered dogs are equally affectionate companions; intact dogs can develop behavior problems.

Neutering males reduces roaming and the potential for aggression. Spaying females frees them of the inconveniences of estrus and subsequent courting by male dogs. It also prevents uterine and ovarian cancer. In addition, spaying before the first heat cycle nearly eliminates the risk of mammary cancer.

Reputable professional breeders produce only a very few extraordinary dogs, and then only to improve the breed. Most professional breeders are strong proponents of altering pet dogs, and many require pet-quality puppies be sterilized.

Puppy mills are shops of horror that make their bloody profit by mass-producing damaged, inferior puppies. Adult dogs are confined in tiny wire cages, and rarely allowed out. They relieve themselves on the wire floor and stand and live in the mess. Health care is poor or nonexistent; adults are kept solely to breed, and females are bred every heat cycle until they wear out and are then destroyed. Puppies are sold in bulk to chain pet stores without socialization, so they make extremely poor pets. Many have infectious diseases or genetic disorders from improper health and breeding standards, and often such puppies die before they reach adulthood.

Unfortunately, there are many irresponsible uninformed people breeding dogs. Some jump into breeding without adequate preparation or knowledge. If I can't convince you not to breed your dog, then at least do it in an intelligent and humane fashion. Read books, quiz your veterinarian, and most importantly, study with a reputable breeder who knows firsthand the pitfalls and demands of breeding. Think ahead: competition is fierce; what will you do if the puppies can't be sold? Do you want to risk placing them in less-than-desirable homes, or will you be able to keep them yourself? Please, don't add to the litter problem. A staggering four out of every litter of five ends up a victim of abandonment, starvation and disease, or relinquishment to a shelter. That puppy ecstatically licking your face is the lucky fifth. Before you permit the suffering to continue, please listen; the clock's still ticking.

MYTH: "Fixing Prince/Princess will make the dog fat and lazy. " **TRUTH:** Dogs, like people, get fat by overeating and not exercising enough.

MYTH: "It matures the dog to have one litter before spaying." **TRUTH:** There's no scientific or medical evidence that having a litter is good for your pet.

MYTH: "I fix the mutts, but King/Queen's a purebred." **TRUTH:** Twenty-five percent of all dogs left at shelters are purebreds that no one wanted.

MYTH: "King's getting old, and I want one of his puppies before he dies." **TRUTH:** Genetics is an inexact science; no puppy, not even King's son, will be just like him.

MYTH: "It's educational for my children to witness the miracle of birth." **TRUTH:** Children learn that puppies can be created and discarded as it suits us. Instead, check with your veterinarian; they often have films available for viewing. Emphasize the real miracle, which is life; teach your children that preventing the births of some pets saves the lives of others.

Dog Laws

In most regions, animal control authorities are sanctioned to seize biting dogs or dogs proven to be incorrigible nuisances. Owners have the right to be notified before the dog is seized or destroyed and given a chance to argue in court that the dog shouldn't be destroyed. You may lose your right to notice if the dog is unlicensed or running at large.

Many places require dogs to wear license tags at all times. All communities require proof of rabies vaccination, since that is also a human health risk. Leash laws require dogs to be on a leash and under human control whenever off of their owner's property. Loose running dogs may be impounded by the animal shelter, and the owner fined. Dogs at pounds are either reclaimed by owners, adopted, sold (usually to research labs), or destroyed. Many facilities can't keep animals longer than three to seven days.

Due to concerns over dangerous dogs, some breeds like Pit Bulls and similar types of dogs are banned in some places. Insurance companies also may decline to cover those who keep dog breeds consider at risk for biting.

"Even a dog knows the difference between being tripped over, and being kicked."
Oliver Wendell Holmes

Before adopting your dog, or moving to a new community, find out what types of laws may affect your canine companion.

Have you made arrangement for someone to care for your dog in the event of your illness or death? By law, a dog is considered property and can't inherit. Instead of leaving property or money to your dog, leave any monies necessary for the care of your dog in trust with a guardian named in your will, and specify that the funds be used solely for the dog. Consult a lawyer for specifics.

In many cities, it's become nearly impossible to find decent rental property that accepts well-mannered dogs, especially canines over a certain size. Offer to pay a security deposit; provide written references from previous landlords and obedience schools; suggest a face-to-face meeting with your dog for an evaluation; and agree to abide by equitable limitations (pooper-scooper and leash restrictions). Never sign a lease that retains a "no pets" clause. Have such clauses removed or amended to protect you from a landlord's change of heart or a change in apartment ownership.

What about cruelty? Definitions are not always specific, but anyone with a modicum of common decency knows when a person has exceeded the bounds. The humane societies and enforcement organizations depend on notification from the public for instances of cruelty. Most animal protection laws are enacted and enforced at the state level. Some cities and counties also pass local ordinances. If you know of or have good reason to suspect instances of animal mistreatment, talk to your local humane association officials.

One night in 1888, a mutt wandered into the Albany, New York, post office. Owney liked to ride trains, and often snuck on board mail shipments. A tag attached to his collar read, "To all who may greet this dog, Owney is his name. He is the pet of 100,000 mail clerks in the United States. Treat him kindly and speed him on his journey, across ocean and land." Owney wandered from Canada to Alaska and Mexico and stowed away on a mail ship to Japan. He was honored by the Mikado and received an award from the Emperor. From Japan, Owney traveled to China and beyond. Postal workers all over the world attached medals and tags (1,017 in all) to his collar. Today, Owney can be seen in the Smithsonian Institute in Washington, D.C.

The Traveling Dog

A health certificate with proof of recent vaccinations is required when traveling with your dog to another state, province, or country. Overseas restrictions also apply: permits must be applied for several weeks in advance, and 4- to 6-month quarantines are often necessary. Your dog may also be required to be microchipped and be current on parasite prevention and vaccinations. Not all airlines accept pets. Service dogs travel in the cabin with their partners, and ESA (Emotional Support Animals) may be allowed depending on the carrier. Small pet dogs may be allowed as carryon, if the carrier fits under the seat, but you'll be charged an additional cost and there's a limitation on numbers allowed in the cabin. Larger dogs in crates are shipped as extra baggage in the belly of the plane and may be restricted by hot or cold weather when allowed to fly. Traveling by car is generally more convenient and comfortable for your dog, but many hotels and motels won't accept pets, or may require a hefty pet deposit. Rules and regulations are subject to change, so call ahead before making travel plans with your dog.

THE DOG BOUTIQUE

Dog houses have gone beyond the simply practical; they now reach for the ultimate in fashion. There are decorated canvas tepees, fiberglass igloos (insulated with nitrogen), log cabins, and solar houses with built-in drainage, heat pumps, and air-conditioners, and even houses with flip-top roofs for those nice, sunny dog-day afternoons. And if your dog becomes bored with the view, you can install a window (dog level, of course) in the backyard fence. Some dogs even have their own hot tubs and personal masseurs to ease the aches and pains of arthritis.

A variety of beds is available as well if the old blanket in the corner isn't good enough anymore. The modern pampered pooch can choose from heated water beds (wonderful for arthritic canines), cedar-stuffed pillows to deter fleas naturally, bunk beds (with attached ladder), day beds complete with coordinated dust ruffle, and even hammocks.

Likewise, dog bowls come in all colors, shapes, and sizes, and can be personalized with your pet's name and portrait. Special bowls are designed to keep fluffy ears from dragging in the food; heated bowls keep water from freezing during the winter; water and food dispensers make self-feeding easy. Trendy foods may be the vogue but hot advertising isn't always science-based, so check with a veterinarian to be sure they're safe. And don't forget the canine caterer to celebrate birthdays and obedience school graduation parties.

The utilitarian leather collar, harness, and leash are old hat; today, the "dogue-in-vogue" has a choice of leather or fabric, with rhinestones (or real stones) and even solar-powered collars that light up so the fashionable dog can be seen on evening walks. They come in every color, even Day-Glo, to make accessorizing that perfect look a little easier.

You can dress your dog with clothes promoting his (or your) favorite football team. And what sports fanatic would be caught dead without a matching hat cut to fit around canine ears and doggy chins? Rainwear makes it possible for dogs to play in wet weather without getting fur coats damp.

There are backpacks for dogs to carry their own weight, and front packs for terrier-toting. If you crave togetherness, why not take your dog to camp?

Vacations designed to take along your pet offer obedience classes, doggy games such as fly-ball, swimming, Frisbee, and general dog enjoyment. The agility course, where you must do everything your dog does, is a special favorite. There are also seminars on dog behavior, trick and obedience training, and even bereavement counseling.

Check out pet product stores in your neighborhood or online for a host of other dog paraphernalia. You can have portraits of your fur-kid painted, or printed on your own clothing, and find breed-specific products to shout your Cavalier or rescue love to the world. Today, dog lovers can pamper their canine family members in countless ways. Just be sure your dog enjoys the products, too.

CANINE CARE

All veterinarians are qualified to treat your dog, but charges and specializations vary. Just as important is the doctor's personality, which should inspire confidence and trust in both you and your pet. The best recommendations come from other dog owners. Be as careful in selecting a veterinarian as you were choosing your pet; after all, your dog's health is at stake. Acupuncture, herbal therapy, chiropractic and behavior help, as well as dozens of veterinary specialists are available for your dog.

Veterinary medicine constantly improves, and information quickly becomes obsolete. The following material is meant only as a guide. Find detailed care and behavior advice in the FURTHER READING resources (page 153). Consult your veterinarian for the most current information.

THE HEALTHY DOG

Have your puppy examined as soon as you get her. Puppies are particularly susceptible to disease and are vaccinated by a series of booster shots two to three weeks apart (just like human babies), with the first given at six to eight weeks. Once the series has been completed, repeated vaccinations every one to three years protect adult dogs thereafter.

Routine Vaccinations

Your puppy should be vaccinated against common canine diseases. *Distemper* is a deadly viral disease affecting a dog's respiratory, intestinal, and central nervous systems; symptoms include yellowish diarrhea, thick discharge from the eyes and nose, and seizures. *Infectious hepatitis* affects the liver, and *leptospirosis* attacks the digestive tract, liver, and kidneys. *Infectious tracheobronchitis* (kennel cough) is a respiratory disease that causes chronic coughing, and may be contracted if your dog is boarded or visits dog parks. Both *parvovirus* and *coronavirus* can be deadly to puppies; symptoms include bloody diarrhea, vomiting, and severe dehydration. *Rabies* acts on the nervous system and results in paralysis and death. Vaccination for rabies is required by law since it can affect people. All these diseases are extremely contagious, yet easily preventable with proper vaccinations.

Altering Your Dog

Dogs are usually altered at six to nine months of age; some professionals delay sterilization to allow physical development of show or performance dogs. However, some programs provide sterilization as early as six weeks (or two pounds) especially for shelter dogs. Surgery is performed under general anesthetic; some dogs are sore for a day or two afterward, and others exhibit no tenderness at all. Puppies bounce back more quickly than adult dogs from the procedure.

A *spay* or ovariohysterectomy removes the female reproductive organs. A small incision is made on the dog's shaved and sterilized abdomen, then the Y-shaped uterus and ovaries are drawn out, tied off, and detached from inside the lower abdomen. Stitches are removed in seven to ten days.

Neutering or castration removes the testicles from the male's scrotal sac. The testicles descend into the scrotum at about ten days after birth. An incision is made in the shaved, sterilized skin of the penis just forward of the scrotum. The testicles are expressed, drawn out, and removed through this one small incision.

Sometimes testicles don't descend, and these cryptorchid dogs have a higher risk of testicular cancer and should always be neutered. Abdominal incisions are necessary to locate retained testicles. Stitches are removed in seven to ten days. Sterilization is often a requirement of shelter adoptions. Many agencies provide certificates for reduced-cost surgeries that most veterinarians gladly honor.

Common External Parasites

Most dogs get external parasites from contact with other infested dogs. *Mange* is caused by demodectic or sarcoptic mites that burrow beneath the dog's skin. Infestation causes itchy sores and hair loss, sometimes serious skin infections, and rarely death.

Ear mites live inside the ear canal, and feed by piercing the skin and sucking lymph. A black, tarry exudate forms inside the ear. Mites contribute to infection by causing irritation and inflammation.

Flies bite and torture, leaving ear tips scabbed and crusty. Flies also lay eggs in dirty or infected ears and skin, and the resulting maggots eat away the dog's

decayed flesh and can severely damage and even kill your dog.

Lice cause intense itching and are spread from contact with an infected animal. The *flea* is the top complaint of pet owners and primarily causes allergic reactions (scratching), and transmits *tapeworms*.

Ticks are bloodsucking parasites that attach to the skin like tiny balloons. Ticks cause painful lesions and spread diseases like *canine ehrlichiosis*, *Lyme disease*, *tick paralysis*, and *Rocky Mountain spotted fever*. External parasites can be eliminated and controlled with proper administration of preventive medications.

Poison!

Be extremely careful with insecticides, cleaning compounds, and any other chemicals. Sweet-tasting antifreeze may lure a dog to drink, but destroys kidneys, and quickly brings death. Signs of poisoning may include abdominal pain, diarrhea or vomiting, lack of coordination, drunken behavior, convulsions, or difficulty breathing. If you suspect poisoning, call your veterinarian for instructions on specific action.

Common Internal Parasites

Dogs get *tapeworms* from swallowing infected fleas or from eating wild animals. Flea control prevents most tapeworm infestation and recurrence. Tapeworm segments look like dried grains of rice that stick to the anal area of your dog's fur.

Most internal parasites are contracted when a dog licks or sniffs contaminated ground. Puppies often get worms from their mother before birth or as they nurse. *Hookworms* cause weight loss, severe anemia, and often death in puppies. *Roundworms* live in the stomach or intestines and look like strings of spaghetti when vomited or passed in the stool; in large numbers they cause intestinal damage and prevent food digestion.

Whipworms produce diarrhea, anemia, weight loss, and weakness. *Coccidiosis* is a protozoan infection prompting bloody diarrhea and dehydration and can cause severe debilitation in puppies. *Giardia* is contracted by drinking infected water and also causes diarrhea. Intestinal parasites are eliminated and prevented with proper veterinary treatment.

Canine heartworms are blood parasites transmitted by mosquitoes from dog to dog. They swim in the bloodstream as larva (microfilaria), then mature and plug the heart, ultimately causing death. Several preventatives are available. Your veterinarian can help you decide which option is best for your pet.

Grooming removes dead hair and loose dander, reduces shedding, prevents painful mats, and stimulates and distributes natural oils. Many breeds demand special coat care, but you can provide basic bathing, combing and brushing for your dog. If you need a professional groomer's help, inspect the premises for cleanliness and professionalism, and don't hesitate to ask questions. Ask if tranquilizers are used, since they have potential risks, and should only be used when a veterinarian is on the premises. Go by word of mouth to find a reputable, knowledgeable groomer.

OTHER CANINE HEALTH CONCERNS

It's estimated that 25 percent of all dog disorders are related to seasonal *allergies*. Allergic skin is the equivalent of hay fever in people; instead of sneezing with runny nose and eyes, the allergic pet itches. Many dogs react to flea saliva, and it takes only one bite to set off an allergic reaction.

Bloat (gastric dilatation volvulus) primarily affects large deep-chested dogs, causing the stomach to swell or twist. Symptoms include restlessness, salivation and drooling, unsuccessful attempts to vomit, and a distended abdomen. Without immediate treatment, painful death quickly occurs.

Diabetes mellitus results when the pancreas doesn't produce enough insulin. Excessive fat can suppress insulin production, and overweight dogs may become diabetic as a direct result of being fat. Without insulin to move glucose into the cells of the body, diabetic dogs can't metabolize food; their appetite increases, but they lose weight. Eventually, the body turns to other fuel sources, and begins burning its own fat and muscle tissue (catabolism). Animals that have progressed to catabolism can rarely be saved. The diabetic dog often has *cataracts*, increased drinking, eating, and urination habits, and dramatic weight loss. Treatment is insulin injections with exercise and dietary management.

When the brain's electrical impulses "short circuit" normal neural processes, seizures may result. *Epilepsy* is a common clinical problem requiring medical management in small animals.

Heatstroke occurs when the dog becomes overheated. Dogs left in closed cars are prime candidates. Signs include shallow, rapid respiration, a rapid heartbeat, and a temperature above 104°F (40°C). Cool the dog as quickly as possible (spray with cool water) and get him to a veterinarian immediately.

Hip dysplasia is a condition in which the hip socket and head of the femur fit improperly, and results in lameness. Signs include hip pain, a limping or wavering gait, a hopping run, and difficulty when rising. Hip dysplasia ranges from severe to minor and may be inherited in certain dog breeds. Surgery can correct

severe forms of the dysplasia, and medication may give relief to minor discomfort.

Hot spots are a common problem occurring most often in the summer, especially in heavy-coated dogs. A round, red, hairless area develops on the skin. The area may emit clear fluid or pus. By chewing at it, dogs aggravate the area, and the painful infection quickly spreads. Hot spots must be treated immediately, or they will become severe.

Pancreatitis (inflammation of the pancreas) commonly occurs in under-exercised, overweight dogs (usually over age two) that are habitually fed a diet of fatty foods, such as table scraps. Symptoms include diarrhea, nausea, and vomiting after eating.

Periodontal disease affects almost all adult dogs by age four. This silent destroyer may affect your dog's heart, liver, and kidneys with severe problems. An affected dog may have bad breath, and the pain will make him stop eating, salivate, and show much distress. Regular brushing of teeth (kits are available) and an annual veterinary cleaning are recommended.

Treating the Sick Dog

Pain, fever, and behavior changes are the earliest signs of ill health in dogs. The best way to recognize illness is to be familiar with your dog's healthy behavior. Consult a veterinarian any time you suspect a problem; better a false alarm than a dead dog.

A very fast heart rate indicates fever, anemia, shock, and any number of other problems. Normally the heart beats seventy to 130 times a minute in a resting dog (the smaller the dog, the faster the rate.) Take a

dog's pulse by placing fingers or palm on her chest just behind and level with the left elbow.

Elimination habits are excellent indications of health and illness. Normal urine is clear yellow, and feces are usually brown and well formed. Foul smelling and/or loose stools, or stools containing mucous or blood (black, tarry stools) are abnormal. Persistent diarrhea or constipation, or changes in the amount or frequency of urination are all indications of potential illness that should be addressed by a veterinarian.

Certainly, we mourn our pets, but they grieve for us as well. Greyfriars Bobby (right) held watch over his master's grave in Edinburgh's historic Greyfriars churchyard for fourteen years until his death.

When Hachiko's human died, all of Japan learned of the faithful Akita that returned to the train station each day at five o'clock to search for his beloved master. The Japanese government erected a statue (below) on the spot where Hachiko kept his ten-year vigil. If there's any justice, all faithful dogs are in death finally reunited with their humans.

Emergencies

Injured dogs may bite even a beloved human out of fear or pain. Muzzle an injured dog for safety, using a long gauze bandage, necktie or other soft cloth. Loop the material around the dog's muzzle and knot snugly over his nose. Bring the ends down under the chin and tie again; then pull the ends back around the dog's head and knot behind his ears.

Whenever a dog stops breathing, time is of the essence. Clear the dog's mouth, check for foreign bodies, and remove them if possible. Place your lips over the dog's nose, and gently blow for three seconds.

Repeat every two to three seconds, up to 15 or 20 breathes per minute until he starts breathing again.

If his heart has stopped, perform cardiopulmonary resuscitation (CPR), alternating chest compressions with rescue breathing. Place the dog on his side on a firm surface. Put your palm over the dog's chest immediately behind his elbow, with your other palm on top; press firmly, then quickly release. Repeat every second, five times in a row, and alternate with one breath.

Medicating Your Dog

Hiding pills in a dog's food doesn't always work. To pill a dog, grasp his muzzle firmly with your left hand. Curl your palm across the top of his muzzle so your thumb and index (or middle) finger encircle his muzzle and fit behind each upper canine tooth. Pressing gently on the dog's lips should cause his lower jaw to open; gently squeezing a finger against the roof of his mouth also works. Insert the pill way back on the center of the tongue, then close and hold the mouth shut while stroking his throat. Dogs often lick their noses after swallowing. If the dog spits the pill out, try again until you're successful.

To give liquid medicine, tilt the head to a 45° angle, then insert the applicator nozzle (dropper or syringe) into the dog's cheek pouch at the corner of the mouth. Keep the head elevated and administer additional medication only after he swallows the initial amount.

Normal adult dog body temperature ranges from 101° to 102.5°F (38° to 39°C). To take your dog's temperature, lubricate a rectal thermometer with mineral oil or Vaseline, place dog in standing position, lift the tail, and insert thermometer into the anus. Leave in place for about three minutes before reading.

The Geriatric Dog

As veterinary health care improves, pets live longer, healthier lives. The dog's average life span is twelve years, but smaller dogs often live longer. Although older pets must live with afflictions of age, you can prevent some problems during your dog's senior years to prolong a cherished friend's life.

Arthritis occurs commonly in older dogs, stiffening joints and making movement painful. Pain is made worse by cold, a sudden change in the weather, or heavy exercise. There is no known cure, but prescription medication may make your pet more comfortable.

Cancer is common in older pets. Breast cancer may affect older, intact female dogs. Skin tumors and oral tumors are just as dangerous. If you find a lump or bump, don't wait—see your veterinarian immediately.

Heart disease affects a third of all older dogs. Congestive heart failure is seen in 75 percent of all dogs over the age of nine. Early signs often include exercise intolerance, shortness of breath, and coughing. In later stages, the dog may lose weight, have fainting spells, and swell with fluid. Without treatment, the dog will eventually die.

Hypothyroidism is caused when the thyroid gland fails to secrete enough thyroid hormone, resulting in an inhibited metabolic rate; symptoms include hair loss along with recurrent skin infections, listlessness and depression, weight gain and

obesity, and also problems staying warm. Treatment consists of thyroid-hormone replacement medication.

The older dog may seem moody and disoriented as her senses become less acute. Eyesight dims, hearing weakens, things just don't smell as good as they used to, so appetite may flag. She may also have trouble controlling bowel or bladder function or remembering to let you know she needs a potty break. Veterinary medicine has made extraordinary advances, but treatment of an aging animal aims to ensure the quality of life, not just prolong it. Sometimes euthanasia is the most merciful choice.

The oldest dog on record was an Australian cattle dog named Bluey that lived 1910-1939 to twenty-nine years, five months.

Euthanasia

Puppies are born; they grow old; they die. Tragic accidents may take them too soon; they may drift away in the gentle sleep of old age; or they may linger in pain, begging silently for relief with suffering, questioning eyes.

When sickness or injury consumes your dog and there is little hope for recovery; when he knows his fight is done, and only a nameless yearning remains; when selfishly sustaining his life merely prolongs pain; the determination to end his suffering is a decision only you, as his best friend, can make.

Euthanasia answers the sick dog's yearning with a single painless needle prick. Veterinarians often allow you to remain and comfort your dog as the medication is administered. You loved your dog best in life; that same love will tell you when it's time to end his pain. Have faith in your love; it's all your pet ever wanted, and he needs that love now more than ever.

No other will ever take a cherished dog's place, but the sadness you feel upon your pet's death will grow sweeter with time. By and by, honor your dog's memory by opening your heart to another. So many yearn to be somebody's dog—love like yours should not be wasted.

Four:
Gallery of Breeds

CHOOSING YOUR DOG

Now comes the hard part: which dog is right for you? A cute puppy, or a settled adult? The predictable temperament and striking features of a purebred, or a robust mix? Dogs vary from pony- to pocket-sized, Whippet-thin to burly. They have foxy or accordion mugs, and tails that are long and thin, short and stout, curled, twisted, or nonexistent. Whatever your preference, a dog that's perfect for you is just waiting to be found.

Choose a breed that best fits your lifestyle. Honest breeders and rescues are willing to discuss potential problems as well as good points; they'll tell you about grooming and exercise requirements, temperament and trainability, and any breed-prone health problems.

If you aren't allowed to inspect the facilities, run! They may be hiding inadequate housing or care. A good breeder or rescue group will be as concerned about your qualifications to provide a good home as you are to obtain a healthy, happy pet. Expect to be asked pointed questions and answer them honestly.

That's About the Size of It!

The tallest breeds are the Great Dane and Irish Wolfhound, but the heaviest are the Old English Mastiff and Saint Bernard. Acromegaly (giantism) is a common mutation that produces massive bones and muscles; facial skin grows out of proportion, producing the wrinkly, jowly appearance of the Bloodhound.

(Left) Borzoi.

The smallest breeds are miniature versions of the larger breeds. Examples include the Yorkshire Terrier, Chihuahua, and Toy Poodle. Miniature animals' heads are proportionally large to accommodate a normal-size brain, but otherwise they're just small versions of larger breeds. Achondroplasia (dwarfism) causes bones to grow into curved, stunted limbs, as in the Basset Hound and Dachshund; early cessation of facial bone growth produces the pug nose, large head, and stubby paws found in Bulldogs.

A variety of dog sports are available for any mix or purebred dog.

Dog Associations

A dog association is a national organization that registers dogs, keeps records of their ancestry in pedigrees, publishes breed standards, sponsors dog shows and events, and determines who will judge them. Kennels are individual establishments that strive to produce the "ideal" dog of a given breed. These dogs then compete in conformation and performance trials sanctioned by the dog association in which that dog is registered. The goal is to determine which dog is closest to the standard of perfection in looks, temperament and/or performance.

Kennels and sometimes individuals hold membership in local or national dog clubs, which in turn are members of one or more dog associations. There are several kinds of dog clubs: all-breed clubs, specialty breed clubs (a single breed), and the performance clubs. Examples include obedience, tracking, field trial, hunting test, herding, coonhound, and lure coursing.

There are a number of dog associations. Breed standards vary from association to association, and not all dog associations recognize the same dog breeds. Registration does not guarantee the quality of a dog, only that both parents were the same breed. However, registered dogs can prove their quality by earning titles, and dog parents with titles usually produce high-quality puppies.

There are about 400 distinct breeds of purebred dogs in the world. The American Kennel Club (AKC) currently recognizes 193 dog breeds; the United Kennel Club (UKC) recognizes 300; and the Canadian Kennel Club (CKC) registers 215 breeds. AKC emphasizes conformation, while the UKC stresses performance and working-dog breeds.

There's simply not enough space to do justice to all the dog breeds of the world. The following gallery section offers only fun, brief descriptions for many popular favorites. Contact the organizations below for detailed descriptions, standards, and histories of recognized breeds, and for location of clubs and breeders.

American Kennel Club (AKC)
http://www.akc.org/

American Rare Breed Association
http://www.arba.org

Australian National Kennel Council
http://ankc.org.au

Canadian Kennel Club
http://www.ckc.ca

Federation Cynologique Internationale
http://www.fci.be/en

Kennel Club of India
http://www.kennelclubofindia.org

Kennel Union of Southern Africa
http://www.kusa.co.za

New Zealand Kennel Club
http://www.nzkc.org.nz

The Kennel Club
http://www.thekennelclub.org.uk

United Kennel Club
http://www.ukcdogs.com

GALLERY

Size key: Height at the shoulder

Small = 15 inches (37.5cm) or less
Medium = 16 to 22 inches (40 to 55cm)
Large = above 23 inches (57.5cm)

Generally, hounds are rather independent, and like to roam; their barks and bays make them a bit noisy around the house. Most spaniels, retrievers, and pointers are too friendly to make good watchdogs; Weimaraners, Chesapeake Bay Retrievers, and American Water Spaniels are the exceptions. Guard dogs have high energy, meaning they require lots of exercise; they're quick to learn, but often stubborn. Draft dog breeds are generally quiet and docile, and easy to train and live with. Most terriers are small, very active dogs that need much attention; they like to bark, making them excellent watchdogs. Herding dogs have high energy, are easy to train and live with, and are devoted. Sled dogs may bark at intruders but are so friendly they'd probably show a burglar where the silver is hidden, and even help load it in his car.

Affenpinscher: This small compact dog is covered with black (usually) wiry fur. Affenpinscher means "monkey dog," and this dog's flat, whiskery face, bushy eyebrows, and round dark eyes are indeed a bit simian. He is generally a quiet, devoted little dog. Picture pg. 131.

Afghan Hound: The Afghan is a large, dignified-looking sighthound (bred to chase prey by sight) with a stunning coat of long, beautiful, silky fur that requires regular grooming. The aristocratic Afghan tends to think for herself but makes a wonderful companion. Picture pg. 35.

Airedale Terrier: The "King of Terriers" is the largest terrier, with a long, flat head, powerful jaws, and hard, dense wiry fur in shades of brown, black, and tan. Originally bred in the nineteenth century to control the otter population on the Aire River in Yorkshire, the Airedale loves water. This dog is sweet tempered with a dignified aloofness. Picture pg. 131.

Akita: This large dog has a bear-like head, curled tail, and thick medium-length fur. Her origins lie in old Japan, where Akitas were used to hunt large animals such as bear and deer. The Akita is a very loving, faithful, and fastidious dog that needs firm training and regular exercise; she is sometimes aggressive toward other dogs. Pictures pg. 168, 131.

Alaskan Malamute: Malamutes are the largest of sled dogs. The wolf-like head has a distinctive white cap or mask, and his thick fur makes him a heavy year-round shedder. Powerfully built and intelligent, Malamutes are also extremely clean and very fond of children. Picture pg. 131.

American Eskimo, Standard and Miniature: The American Eskimo, nicknamed "The Dog Beautiful," may be either small or medium size and looks like a miniature Samoyed. This curious, gregarious, occasionally headstrong dog wants to be in on everything.

American Staffordshire Terrier: This handsome, impressive, medium-sized dog tragically is best known for illegal use in dog fights. In the United Kennel Club, the breed is known as the American Pit Bull Terrier. Although often aggressive with dogs, they're usually gentle, loyal, and extremely affectionate with people when correctly socialized. Picture pg. 132.

Australian Shepherd: Aussies are gorgeous medium size, long-furred dogs resembling small Collies, but with almost no tail. They are an extremely intelligent working breed. Picture pg. 132

Australian Terrier: Here's a small terrier with attitude resembling the Cairn terrier but with a silky topknot and longish body. He's a confident dog that's easy to train, and enjoys apartment living or work on the farm.

Australian Terrier

Basenji: The Basenji is an ancient dog, native to North Africa. She is a medium size dog with pricked ears, a wrinkled, intelligent face, curled tail, and short, very fine, sleek fur. The Basenji cleans herself like a cat; she doesn't bark, but chortles, yodels, and sometimes screams. Basenjis make endearing, courageous, playful yet gentle pets. Pictures pg. 98, 132.

Basset Hound: This is a hefty, medium size, deep-voiced dog with a smooth, short coat. He moves ponderously on very short legs, making him an excellent tracker. Bassets have extremely long ears that "sweep the morning dew" and are gentle, good-mannered dogs. Picture pg. 132.

Beagle: This cheerful little hound, known for her hunting abilities since Elizabethan times, may be either small or medium size, and has never met a stranger. She likes lots of running room, and lives for sniffing. Picture pg. 133.

Bearded Collie: The medium size Beardie wears a quizzical expression on her bearded face and is full of high energy and spirits. This long-coated dog makes a stable, self-confident, devoted family pet. Picture pg. 133.

Bedlington Terrier: A lamb look alike, the Bedlington is a hardy, medium size dog. Developed by miners in nineteenth-century England, he was used to eliminate vermin from the mines. His pear-shaped head and mild, gentle expression are endearing; he walks with a mincing springy step, and has thick, soft stand-up fur. Picture pg. 133.

Belgian Shepherds: The Groenendael is a large, solid black dog that looks like a long-haired German Shepherd. The Tervuren looks similar but with fawn to mahogany fur with black tips. The rare Laekenois has a rough, tan coat; the Malinois (a favorite with military and police) looks like a short-coated German Shepherd. These gorgeous breeds are year-round shedders, highly trainable, always in motion, and not for the faint of heart. Picture pg. 95.

Bernese Mountain Dog: This is a large Mastiff-type black dog with white and tan markings on a wavy, long silky coat. The Berner is an exceptionally faithful, hardy dog that needs human companionship. Picture pg. 133.

Bichon Frise: The sturdy Bichon is a small, bouncy, snow-white powder-puff of a dog with black merry eyes; her full beard makes her look like Santa Claus. The Bichon Frise does not shed, but her silky hair requires regular grooming. Once a pampered favorite of European courtiers, the Bichon is smart and devoted—an excellent pet. Picture pg. 134.

Black And Tan Coonhound: The Black and Tan is a big, active muscular dog with short, sleek hair, and a friendly but businesslike attitude. He hunts by scent, then "barks up" or gives voice the moment his quarry is treed, and he is happiest when working. Picture pg. 134.

Bloodhound: Bloodhounds are powerful, large, formidable tracking dogs, with characteristic loose facial skin that hangs in deep folds. Puppies have been known to trip over their own ears. This is a reserved but good-tempered dog that's gentle with children. Picture pg. 134.

Border Collie: Originally a Scottish herding dog, this medium to large size, extremely intelligent, loyal worker resembles a small Collie with a broad muzzle. Pictures pg. 93, 114, 134.

Border Terrier: She is an active, tireless and plucky small dog that comes in a red, grizzle and tan, blue and tan or a wheaten short coat that's harsh and weather resistant. She is one of the most affectionate of the terriers and tends to be a good-tempered dog that makes a fine pet. Picture pg. 135.

Borzoi (Russian Wolfhound): The elegant Borzoi is a large sighthound with long fur. He was developed in Russia in the thirteenth century. This quiet, gentle aristocrat is easy to train and makes an excellent companion. Picture pg. 112.

Boston Terrier: The small "Boston Gentleman" is a saucy scamp with boundless energy that stands up to anything. She resembles a tiny Boxer, except for the screw tail and distinctive two-tone coat that looks like a tuxedo. Bostons make wonderful house pets; however, they share the breathing problems of all flat-nosed breeds. Picture pg. 135.

Bouvier

Bulldog

Bouvier de Flandres: This large dog's roughly tousled, harsh, wiry fur makes him look like an unshorn giant Schnauzer. Bred as a cattle herder in Flanders, he is spirited and bold, but well behaved and fearless. Picture pg. 117.

Boxer: Boxers are sturdy, medium size, squarely built dogs, with deep facial wrinkles, cropped ears, docked tail, undershot jaw, and short, tight fur. Nineteenth-century German breeders developed the Boxer as a police dog of intelligence and courage. Boxers have a playful temperament; they're wary of strangers but make friends easily. Picture pg. 135.

Briard: This large, hairy dog is often described as a heart wrapped in fur—6 inches (15cm) of straight fur all over that needs lots of grooming. A very ancient French herding and guard dog, today's Briard is an independent, yet devoted pet. Picture pg. 135.

Brittany: The medium size Britt wants to hunt; she is a loving dog with little or no tail, covered with either dark orange and white, or liver and white wavy fur. She is very friendly, wants to please, and is an excellent dog for children. Picture pg. 136.

Brussels Griffon: This small dog has personality plus, and is a little larger than, but otherwise resembles, the Affenpinscher. Popular with nineteenth-century Belgian royalty, the Brussels Griffon is intelligent and independent. Picture pg. 136.

Bulldog: The Bulldog is small to medium in stature, but very broad, powerful, and compact. His massive head is proportionally larger than the rest of the body, and he has a flattened, wrinkled face. Despite a ferocious expression, Bulldogs have kind, dignified natures. A bit smaller with large upright ears, the French Bulldog is one of the sweetest and popular small dogs. Pictures pg. 38, 79, 118-119.

Bullmastiff: This large dog looks like a Boxer on steroids with natural drop ears and long uncropped tail and weighs up to 130 pounds. The short coat comes in red, fawn or brindle. He's a confident, fearless yet docile pet willing to please. Picture pg. 136.

Bull Terrier (and Miniature): This small to medium short haired dog can be all white or any color with white. He has a distinctive egg-shaped head, small dark sunken eyes, erect ears, and a tapered tail and loves affection. Picture pg. 68.

Cairn Terrier: The cheeky Cairn is a small, shaggy, compact dog, with a "weatherproof coat." This charmer is tempted to forge ahead on leash, and prone to barking. Toto from the Wizard of Oz was a Cairn Terrier. Picture pg. 136.

Cavalier King Charles Spaniel: This is the small beguiling dog favored by King Charles II of England and featured in many famous paintings. Large expressive eyes give her an endearing quality. These dogs are willing and even anxious to learn, with low excitability. Picture pg. 137.

Chesapeake Bay Retriever

Chesapeake Bay Retriever: The Chessie is a large gundog that looks similar to a Labrador but with a close-fitting wavy coat. They love the water and enjoy training.

Chihuahua: An ancient Mexican breed, the Chihuahua is a miniature mastiff often weighing less than two pounds (0.9 kg). He has either short, smooth fur or a long, silky coat. Despite a dainty look, he has a fierce, forceful personality and will challenge authority. Pictures pg. 85, 137.

Chinese Crested Dog: This is a very clean small dog. He may be coated—Powderpuff variety with double silky all-over fur—or hairless, with only tufts of fur on the head and face, feet and tail tip. This is an elegant, graceful dog, a playful and devoted pet that is gay and alert. Picture pg. 137.

Chinese Shar-Pei: The sweet, lovable Shar-Pei is of medium or small stature, and is known for extraordinarily wrinkled, loose skin, a hippo-like face, a blue-black tongue,

and a short, bristly coat. (Shar-Pei means "sandy coat.") Originally bred in China as fighting dogs, some Shar-Peis tend to be dog aggressive. Pictures pg. 120-121.

Chinese Shar-Pei

Chow Chow: Chows are large, densely furred Chinese dogs that look like a cross between a lion and a bear. They are known for a blue-black tongue, scowling expression, and tightly curled tail. Chows are dignified, loyal pets with a reputation as one-person dogs. They're often reserved with strangers and sometimes aggressive with other dogs. Picture pg. 122.

Clumber Spaniel: This thoughtful looking, dignified large dog looks like a cross between a Cocker and Basset. He is an active, tireless retriever that moves with a rolling gait. Picture pg. 138.

Cocker Spaniel: The very popular Cocker is a sturdy, small dog with a rounded head, long, elegant ears, and profuse, gorgeous fur. Cockers are merry, laid-back, companionable dogs with a short, docked tail constantly in happy motion. Picture pg. 138.

Collie, Rough and Smooth: The "Lassie" stories popularized this large, strong, active shepherd; he has a distinctive, full, lush coat with a white-maned "collar." The Smooth Collie has a short smooth coat and looks more angular. Pictures pg. 43, 60.

Dachshund: The small, muscular Dachshund has a long, svelte body set on short legs, and is either standard or miniature in size. The coat may be smooth, long, or wire-haired. Originally used to flush badgers out of their holes, the Dachshund is active, very trainable, and occasionally pushy or stubborn. The Dachshund is both clever and courageous, and often gets into trouble just for fun. Early training is a must to keep an upper hand. Pictures pg. 52-53.

Dalmatian: Dalmatians are large dogs with characteristic dark "polka dots" against white, short, smooth hair. They have a long and varied working history and are known for their affinity with horses. Dalmatians are very clean and loyal one-person/family dogs. Pictures pg. 89-90.

Dandie Dinmont Terrier: This hardy, fearless small dog looks like a Dachshund with lots of crisp, soft hair. Dandies need regular grooming; they fit in anywhere. Picture pg. 138.

Doberman Pinscher: The Doberman is a large dog with the agility, strength, and speed of a giant terrier. His head is long and clean, eyes deep and almond shaped, and ears and tail often cropped. He has smooth, close-lying fur. Dobermans are extremely intelligent, loyal, fiercely protective, and devoted family dogs. Picture pg. 138.

Dogue de Bordeaux: This large Mastiff-type breed is the national dog of France. The Dogue has a smooth, short, light-colored coat with black points. Picture pg. 138.

Finnish Spitz: The medium size Finn looks like a fox. Finland's national dog, the Finn is lively and courageous, and an excellent hunter. Barking can be a problem; sensitive and independent, the Finn is easily bored with repetition. Picture pg. 140.

Flat-Coated Retriever: This large dog, a descendant of the Newfoundland, resembles a Labrador Retriever but with moderate-length, flat-lying fur; minimal grooming is required. Dependable and active, this is a heavy tail-wagger. Picture pg. 140.

Foxhound: The Foxhound is a large dog with a fairly long domed head, long pendulous ears, gay tail, and a close, hard, medium-length coat.

Fox Terrier, Smooth and Wire: Fox Terriers are small to medium size white dogs with colored markings. The tail is docked long and held erect, and ears drop forward close to the cheek. The Wire Fox Terrier looks like a small Airedale. This is a gay, lively dog that gets excited at the least provocation. Picture pg. 150.

German Shepherd Dog (Alsatian): This large, noble dog resembles a wolf. He's a heavy shedder year-round and needs lots of exercise. Shepherds thrive on training; they are intelligent, eager to please, loyal, loving, protective, and fearless, yet cautious with strangers. Pictures pg. 66, 140.

German Shorthaired Pointer: This large all-purpose hunter has webbed feet and short water-resistant coat that makes him a standout field and water retriever. His short close coat comes in solid silver or any combination of liver and white (ticked, roan, or spotted). He is a good watchdog that's accepting of approved strangers and gets along well with children and other dogs. Picture pg. 140.

Golden Retriever: The Golden is a large dog with a broad head, moderately long fur, and a kind expression. Goldens crave attention and adore being with people; they'll submit to nearly anything just to be near their owners, and they adore children. Pictures pg. 69-71.

Great Dane: Danes are very large, reaching more than 30 inches (75cm) at the shoulder. This is a muscular dog with a refined Mastiff head, cropped ears, and short, thick, glossy fur. Danes tend to age rather quickly, and a wagging tail can be a bruising experience. Spirited and courageous, friendly and dependable, Danes make excellent pets, but you may go broke feeding them. Picture pg. 139.

Great Pyrenees: The majestic white Pyrenees is a large Mastiff-type dog that often reaches 120 pounds (59kg), and moves with an ambling, rolling gait. He is very muscular and courageously protective, yet gentle and devoted to his family. Picture pg. 145.

Greater Swiss Mountain Dog: This large herding and draft dog looks like a short coated black Saint Bernard. She is a wonderful all-around work dog. Picture pg. 128.

Japanese Chin

Greyhound: The elegant Greyhound is a large, very ancient Egyptian breed. Originally bred as a hunting dog, today the Greyhound is known for speed—up to 35 miles (56km) per hour. She is a quiet and clean pet and is affectionate without fawning. Picture pg. 139.

Ibizan Hound: This large deer-like dog looks like a Greyhound with upright ears that flush with emotion. She has a pink nose and amber eyes. Friendly and active, Ibizans are excellent family dogs and are very healthy.

Irish, Irish & White, and Gordon Setters: Legend holds that the Irish Setter arose "fully formed from among the shamrocks." This large dog has a distinctive, silky, rich chestnut to red coat. He has a puppyish exuberance and zest for life and needs a lot of exercise. The **Gordon Setter** looks similar but is coal black with chestnut markings. The **Irish Red And White Setter** (pg. 123) is similar, but a bit stockier than the others. Picture pg. 139.

Irish Water Spaniel: This large dog, with a coat of crisp tight ringlets, resembles a Standard Poodle with a long, fringeless tail. The Irisher is a one person/family dog, easily taught, eager, and enthusiastic.

Irish Wolfhound: This large dog often reaches 120 pounds (54kg) and resembles a very heavy Greyhound with wiry, rough textured fur in various solid colors. He is a gentle, brave, and dignified dog. Picture pg. 141.

Irish Water Spaniel

Italian Greyhound: The IG is a small sighthound, which can reach speeds of up to 40 miles (64km) per hour. She is intelligent, affectionate, and sensitive, and was a favorite of royalty throughout Europe during the nineteenth century. Picture pg. 144.

Japanese Chin: The Chin is a small, Pug-like dog with long, profuse black and white, or red and white fur. She carries a plumed tail draped over her back and lifts her feet high as she walks. Long a favorite of Japan's emperors, the Chin is a bright, alert, very clean dog that never forgets a friend—or an enemy!

Keeshond: The Keeshond has a dense, ash-gray, easy-care coat. A Dutch breed, this is a most affectionate, lovable dog.

Kerry Blue Terrier: The medium-size Kerry Blue is the national dog of Ireland, and looks a little like the Airedale in shape. He has a distinctive soft, wavy blue-gray coat. Kerries are smart and lovable and make excellent watchdogs; they tend to fight other dogs. Picture pg. 141.

Komondor

Kuvatz

Komondor: This is a large, 120-pound (54kg) dog with an unusual heavy, white, tassel-like corded coat. He looks like a mop on legs. Komondors are self-reliant, protective, earnest, and faithful dogs. Picture pg. 124.

Kuvasz: The Hungarian Kuvasz is a large white dog very similar to the Great Pyrenees. Kuvasz means "protector"; these dogs demonstrate extremely strong protective responses toward children and are slow to make new friends.

Labrador Retriever: Labs are large, black, yellow, or chocolate-colored dogs with dense short coats and a distinctive broad "otter tail" that may bruise you when exuberantly wagged. Labs are strong, active dogs that need minimal grooming, are exceedingly friendly and excellent with children.

Lakeland Terrier: This "big dog in a small package" is a bold character originally bred to work in packs against foxes bent on raiding the sheep. He has a low shedding, hard, wiry coat. Picture pg. 142.

Lhasa Apso: This small, solid Pekingese-like dog has a screw tail carried well over the back, and lots of straight, hard hair, even over the face. Lhasas are watchful, hardy, easily trained, and obedient to those they trust. Picture pg. 126.

Maltese: The fastidious Maltese is a small, solid white dog with long pendant ears, a tail that arches over her back, and lots of silky straight fur that demands much grooming.

Maltese

Labradors come in three colors.

Lhasa Apso

Manchester Terrier: This is a small dog that comes in standard and toy varieties, and resembles a long-tailed tiny Doberman. The Manchester is a wise, intelligent, sleek, and clean little dog. Picture pg. 142.

Mastiff: This is a very large, powerful dog reaching more than 30 inches (75cm) in height, with a square head, short, broad muzzle, and small ears that lie flat and close to the cheek. Mastiffs have short, close-lying fur in various colors, and are good-natured and courageous, yet docile. Picture pg. 142.

Miniature Pinscher: The small "King of Toys" looks like a tiny Doberman, and is a very alert, self-possessed watchdog. He is a bold, loving little dog that has a tendency to show off. Picture pg. 142.

Newfoundland: The Newfie is a 130-pound (59kg) Mastiff-type dog with a moderately long black or bronze coat. He is a heavy shedder. Despite his size, the Newfie has a very gentle, docile nature. Pictures pg. 42, 143.

Norwegian Elkhound: The Norwegian Elkhound is a large, spitz-type dog resembling the Keeshond, but with shorter fur, and is a friendly, energetic dog.

Old English Sheepdog: This large tailless dog has profuse, shaggy gray and white fur that covers the entire body, even the face and eyes; she needs careful and frequent grooming. The Old English has a distinctive ambling gait and a bell-like bark. She is a naturally exuberant and playful dog that demands attention and a daily romp. Picture pg. 143.

Otterhound: No longer employed for hunting otter for which he was bred in medieval England, today this large, joyous affectionate dog makes a fun pet. He's known for a dense shaggy coat, love of swimming, webbed feet, and acute nose.

Papillon: Think of a Japanese Chin with a foxy muzzle, and you get the small Papillon. Ears are frilled and carried like the spread wings of a "papillon," or butterfly. This is a friendly, hardy dog. Picture pg. 143.

Parson Russell Terrier: The PRT (previously called the Jack Russell) is a small, tough, sporty dog that's full of confidence, and has a mostly white coat with tan or black markings. His ears are dark brown and almond shaped, and the docked tail is carried high. Picture pg. 141.

Otter Hound

Pekingese: The small Pekingese was created when a lion "yielded to the caresses of a butterfly." This thick-set, short-legged dog has a wide, flat head and an extremely short, wrinkled nose; long, profuse straight hair cascades over the body, and the tail is carried over the back. Pekes are calm and good tempered; they condescend to strangers but welcome a romp with the family. Picture pg. 143.

Petit Basset Griffon Vendeen: The PBGV is one of the small ancient French hounds and looks somewhat like a rough wirehaired Basset. Most PBGVs are stubborn and tend toward independence and may be hard to train but can be a good family pet. He is a happy extrovert willing to please. Picture pg. 144.

Pharoah Hound: This large red sighthound is one of the oldest of domesticated dogs, tracing her ancestry to at least 3000 BC where she was a favorite of the ancient Egyptians. When excited or happy, the Pharoah "blushes"—her nose and ears turn a deep rosy color. This elegant, striking dog is at once graceful and powerful, and loves to run. Picture pg. 144.

Pomeranian: The Pom is the smallest of the spitz breeds and is a heavy shedder year-round. She is docile yet vivacious. Picture pg. 144.

Poodle (Toy, Miniature, Standard): This active, elegant dog is available in three sizes (small, medium, and large) and a variety of colors. Poodles don't shed, but grooming is necessary to achieve their distinctive appearance. Poodles are very smart and will train you in the blink of an eye, so stay on your toes. Picture pg. 144.

Portuguese Water Dog: This breed was developed to aid fisherman by herding fish into nets, retrieving lost tackle, and carrying messages through the water from ship to ship. She looks somewhat like a Poodle, but in fact has two accepted coat types, either curly or wavy. Typically, she's clipped short all over; or is trimmed in a "lion clip" that leaves the coat long everywhere except the middle, muzzle and hindquarters which are clipped short. Fur comes in black, white, or brown. Picture pg. 145.

Pug: The small Pug looks like a toy Mastiff with a curled tail. Some say the name derives from the Latin *pugnus*, meaning "fist," because his profile resembles a fist. The Pug lives for people and has little or no odor. Picture pg. 145.

Puli: This medium dog resembles the larger mop-coated Komondor, but with rusty black fur and a tail carried over the back. He's an affectionate, home-loving companion that is suspicious of strangers. Picture pg. 75.

Rottweiler

Rhodesian Ridgeback: This is a large dog with a distinctive ridge of hair growing on his back. A clean, easily kept pet, the Rhodesian Ridgeback is rarely noisy and loves children. Picture pg. 145.

Rottweiler: This compact, powerful dog is a large, mostly black, Mastiff-type dog with a broad, wrinkled head, docked tail, and ears that tip forward. She is bold and courageous, self-assured, slow to make friends, and protective of home and family. Pictures pg. 73, 127.

Picture pg. 61.

Greater Swiss Mountain Dog

Saint Bernard: This dog is another very large Mastiff-type with long orange and white fur. She's a heavy year-round shedder. There's also a smooth-haired, short-coated variety. Picture pg. 146.

Saluki: The Saluki is another large sighthound with long silky fur on the ears and tail. He is an ancient northern African and Asian breed, originally used for hunting. The Saluki is very catlike in the way he cleans himself, and is an aloof, one-family dog.

Samoyed: A striking, gorgeous large white or cream-colored spitz-type dog originally bred in Siberia, the Samoyed is a heavy shedder year-round. Samoyeds are excellent watchdogs, yet gentle and companionable. Picture pg. 44.

Schipperke: Schipperkes are small to medium size cobby dogs with a sharp expression and an air of self-importance. Once used as a watchdog on boats, they have a foxy head, a tailless, rounded rump, and a dense, harsh, black coat that forms a mane. The name "little captain" comes from the Flemish word for "skipper." He is very fond of children and will defend house and family against all comers. Picture pg. 147.

Schnauzer (Miniature, Standard, Giant): The medium size Standard Schnauzer is the prototype for the small Miniature and large Giant Schnauzer breeds. Although they look similar but for size, these are three distinct unrelated breeds. Today, she's prized as a house companion. Typically, her tail is docked, and ears are cropped to stand erect; natural ears are drop. She is a fearless protector, intelligent and high-spirited. The Giant Schnauzer sometimes serves as a police dog. Though affectionate, she's not especially eager to please, and always has her own agenda. Picture pg. 147.

Scottish Terrier: The small, thickset, wiry-coated Scottie has short legs, erect pointed ears, and a head that seems too long for his size. Pictures pg. 68, 147.

Shetland Sheepdog: Shelties are small to medium size, extremely intelligent dogs. They look like miniature Collies. Shelties are intensely loyal, affectionate, and responsive, yet reserved with strangers. Picture pg. 147.

Shiba Inu: This small spitz-type dog from Japan has a curled tail, erect ears, and a short thick coat that comes in all colors, with red, red sesame, and black and tan preferred. She was developed as a hunting dog and remains a very active dog with a strong hunting instinct that can be dangerous to small pets. The Shiba is an independent character that's stubborn to train, and can be aggressive with other dogs and aloof with strangers. She's a clean, lively dog that will adapt well to apartment living, and is very affectionate with her people. Picture pg. 148.

Shih Tzu: This small, ancient Chinese dog looks similar to the Pekingese, but has much more facial hair. The Shih Tzu is often called the "chrysanthemum-faced dog" because facial hair grows in all directions. This is a very active, alert dog with an arrogant carriage. Pictures pg. 76, 148.

Siberian Husky: This is a large breed a bit smaller than, but otherwise very similar in appearance to the Alaskan Malamute. Developed as a sled dog, he is a heavy shedder year-round. Huskies are naturally friendly, gentle, very alert, quite clean, and sometimes independent. Pictures pg. 78, 148.

Skye Terrier: The small Skye has short legs and long body like the Dachshund, and has straight long fur hanging to the ground and over the face. He is generally a one-person dog. The Skye is distrustful of strangers. Picture pg. 148.

Soft-Coated Wheaten Terrier: The Wheaten has been known for at least 200 years in Ireland, and some believe her to be an ancestor of the Kerry Blue Terrier. She is a medium size dog with soft, medium length wheat colored fur. She has a mild manner for a terrier and is a sensitive dog, but self-confident and gay with those she knows. Picture pg. 146.

Staffordshire Bull Terrier: This short-coated medium size dog is a Hercules for his size, yet agile and active. He was developed early in the 19th century when dog fighting was the vogue. This is a courageous dog, intelligent and strong, and affectionate with family and friends. Picture pg. 146.

Tibetan Spaniel: This medium size dog arose in the same place and time as the Lhasa Apso, and in fact looks a bit like a short haired Lhasa Apso. She is a short-legged long bodied dog with curled tail, drop spaniel ears, and short face. She barks a lot, and is a great watchdog, but needs consistent training from puppyhood to combat her stubborn attitude. Older children are fine, but this breed may not appreciate unpredictable small children. Picture pg. 146.

Tibetan Terrier: The Tibby is a medium size dog that carries his tail over his back and has a profuse soft double coat in any color that falls over the face. He's rather square and not low to the ground. He's a quiet, happy and friendly companion and a wonderful choice for the family dog. Picture pg. 149.

Vizsla: Sometimes called the Hungarian Pointer, this large dog looks like a smaller rusty-gold version of the Weimaraner. The Vizsla is an obedient and affectionate companion.

Weimaraner: The large "gray ghost" is known for her shimmery gray coat, light-colored eyes and effortless movement. Loyal and obedient, she enjoys being in the middle of a family. Picture pg. 57.

Welsh Corgi (Cardigan and Pembroke): These small dogs look like German Shepherds with sawed-off legs; the Pembroke has pointed ears and no tail, while the Cardigan has rounded ears, a full tail, and is a little larger. The Pembroke is known as the dog of the British Royal family. These dogs have big opinions of themselves but are very agreeable house pets that need frequent exercise. Corgis require minimal grooming. Picture pg. 149.

Welsh Springer Spaniel: This medium size dog is one of the most ancient of hunting breeds, traceable back to 250 B.C. The red and white Welsh Springer Spaniel is an excellent water dog with a sensitive nose and is larger and stronger than the Cocker Spaniel but smaller than the English Springer. He's known to be gentle and affectionate with children and other dogs but is reserved with strangers and will act as a guard dog should the occasion arise. Picture pg. 149.

West Highland White Terrier: The small snow-white Westie is shaped somewhere between the Cairn and the Scottish Terrier. A tough, brave, spunky dog originally bred for hunting small animals, the Westie is lively and demanding of attention. An ideal apartment dog, the Westie tends to be a barker and likes to dig, so beware. Picture pg. 150.

Whippet: The Whippet is another medium size Greyhound look-alike. Whippets are elegant, easy-to-train dogs that are small enough to carry. They have an easy-care, short coat. Picture pg. 150.

Xolo.

Wirehaired Pointing Griffon: This is a medium size general purpose hunting dog known for his distinctive harsh wiry double coat. The color typically is steel gray with brown markings. He is a strong swimmer and excellent water retriever. Unlike many hunting dogs, the intelligent Griffon is quick to learn, and wants to please. He makes a great family dog as well as hunting companion. Picture pg. 150.

Xoloitzcuintli: The Xolo (show-low), also known as the Mexican Hairless, resembles an oiled Chihuahua, but ranges from tiny to more than 60 pounds (27kg). Not all Xolos are completely bald. Many Xolos prefer an odd resting posture of butt up, front end down. Xolos have a sweet, sensitive personality and need to be with people. They love to play tricks. Tiny Xolos enjoy perching on shoulders.

Yorkshire Terrier: The Yorkie is a small, very compact dog with erect ears, docked tail, and long, perfectly straight metallic hair. Cuteness allows the highly intelligent Yorkie to manipulate owners into all kinds of concessions. Show dogs need lots of grooming. Yorkies have a devastatingly shrill bark that neighbors don't appreciate. Pictures pg. 91, 150.

AFTERWORD

This book has been a joy to write. I hope the tales and tips, frolics, and facts catalogued in its pages have not only answered many of your questions, but also whetted your appetite to learn more.

The following pages offer another 80+ pictures to celebrate the amazing variety of dog breeds. What's your pick of the litter? I grew up with Shelties, shared my life with amazing German Shepherds, and now adore Bravo, a Bullmastiff mix (see him on page 151).

Learning about *Canis familiaris* is an exciting adventure. Becoming educated about the wonderful world of dogs makes us better caretakers to each impish, playful, devoted furry wonder we welcome into our family.

The dog has trotted the globe and traveled hundreds of centuries with humans, remaining ever faithful. Responsible dog lovers like you will ensure that the dog keeps his envied position: the canine companion, pampered pet, valued partner, and above all, best friend.

Affenpinscher

Alaskan Malamute

Akita

Airedale

Australian Shpeherd

American Staffordshire
Terrier

Basenji

Basset Hound

Bedlington Terrier

Beagle

Bearded Collie

Bernese
Mountain Dog

Bichon Frise

Bloodhound

Border Collie

Black & Tan Coonhound

Border Terrier

Boston Terrier

Briard

Boxer

Brittany

Brussels
Griffon

Cairn Terrier

Bullmastiff

Cavalier
King Charles
Spaniel

Chihuahua
(Longhair & Smooth)

Chinese Crested

Clumber Spaniel

Cocker Spaniel (American)

Doberman Pinscher

Dandie Dinmont
Terrier

Dogue
de Bordeaux

Greyhound

Irish Setter

Gordon Setter

Great Dane

Finnish Spitz

Flat-Coated Retriever

German Shorthaired Pointer

German Shepherd Dog

Jack Russell Terrier

Kerry Blue Terrier

Italian Greyhound

Irish Wolfhound

Lakeland Terrier

Manchester Terrier

Miniature Pinscher

Mastiff

Pekingese

Old English Sheepdog

Newfoundland

Papillon

Petit Basset
Griffon Vendeen

Pomeranian

Pharoah Hound

Poodle

Rhodesian Ridgeback

Great Pyrenees

Portuguese Water Dog

Pug

Staffordshire Bull Terrer

Saint Bernard

Tibetan Spaniel

Soft-Coated
Wheaten Terrier

Schnauzer

Scottish Terrier

Schipperke

Shetland Sheepdog

Siberian Husky

Shi Tzu

Shiba Inu

Skye Terrier

Tibetan Terrier

Welsh Springer Spaniel

Welsh Corgi (Cardigan)

Westhighland
White Terrier

(Wirehaired) Fox Terrier

Wirehaired
Pointing Griffon

Yorkshire Terrier

Whippet

ABOUT THE AUTHOR

Amy Shojai (www.SHOJAI.com) is a certified animal behavior consultant, and the award-winning author of more than 30 bestselling pet books that cover furry babies to old fogies, first aid to natural healing, and behavior/training to Chicken Soupicity. She has been featured as an expert in hundreds of print venues including The New York Times, The Wall Street Journal, Readers' Digest, and Family Circle, as well as television networks such as CNN, and Animal Planet. Amy brings her unique pet-centric viewpoint to public appearances. She is also a playwright and co-author of STRAYS, THE MUSICAL and the author of the critically acclaimed September & Shadow pet-centric thriller series. Amy lives in Texas with her furry muses.

"The more I see of men, the better I like dogs."
Mme. Roland (1754-1793)

FURTHER READING

Dog Facts: The Pet Parent's A-to-Z Home Care Encyclopedia by Amy Shojai

Complete Puppy Care by Amy Shojai

ComPETability: Solving Behavior Problems in Your Multi-DOG Household by Amy Shojai

ComPETability: Solving Behavior Problems in Your CAT-DOG Household by Amy Shojai

Complete Care for Your Aging Dog by Amy Shojai

New Choices in Natural Healing for Dogs and Cats by Amy Shojai

The First-Aid Companion for Dogs and Cats by Amy Shojai

FURRY MUSE
PUBLICATIONS
P.O. Box 1904, Sherman, TX 75091
www.SHOJAI.com

A

Affenpinscher, 116, 119
Afghan Hound, 27, 62, 116
African Painted Dogs, 13, 15, 16
Aggressive Behavior, 26, 45, 86-87, 94, 116, 121
Airedale Terrier, 66, 116
Akita, 116
Alaskan Malamute, 64
Allergies, 107
Altering, 98
American Eskimo, 116
American Kennel Club, 64, 115
American Staffordshire Terrier, 64
American Water Spaniel, 115
American Working Terrier Association, 62
Aristotle, 39
Assistance Dogs, 70, 72
Australian Shepherd, 116
Aztec, 28, 55

B

Barking And Howling, 56, 57, 80, 87, 92, 120
Basenji, 18, 116
Basset Hound, 114, 116
Beagle, 66, 116
Bearded Collie, 117
Bedlington Terrier, 117
Beds, 92, 101
Belgian Malinois, 66, 95, 117
Belgian Shepherd, 117
Bernese Mountain Dog, 117
Bichon Frise, 117
Black And Tan Coonhound, 117
Bloat, 107
Bloodhound, 23, 34, 55, 113, 117
Border Terrier, 117
Borzoi, 27, 62, 117
Boston Terrier, 117
Bouvier De Flandres, 66, 118
Boxer, 49, 57, 117, 118
Breed, 114-115
Breed Clubs, 36
Breeding, 14, 15, 32, 34, 36, 89, 99
Briard, 64, 118
Brittany, 119
Brussels Griffon, 119
Bull Terrier, 35, 120
Bulldog, 23, 45, 119
Bullmastiff, 120
Bush Dog, 19, 25

C

Cairn Terrier, 120
Call Of The Wild, The (London), 43
Canadian Kennel Club, 115
Canidae, Family Of, 11, 13, 14, 23
Canine Companions For Independence, 71
Cape Hunting Dogs, 13, 15, 16
Cardigan Welsh Corgi, 129
Cat Family, 13
Cavalier King Charles Spaniel, 120
Chesapeake Bay Retriever, 115, 120
Chewing, 94
Chihuahua, 23, 28, 71, 114, 120, 130
China, 11, 14, 19, 32, 36, 121
Chinese Crested Dog, 13, 120
Chinese Shar-Pei, 120
Chocolate, as Poison 84
Chow Chow, 121
Clumber Spaniel, 121
Cocker Spaniel, 121
Collie, 27, 43, 60, 71, 117, 121
Coprophagia, 84
Communication, 13, 26, 77, 81, 86
Coyote, 13, 55

D

Dachshund, 15, 60, 81, 114, 121-122, 129
Dalmatian, 29, 122
Dandie Dinmont Terrier, 122
Descartes, Rene, 40
Dhole (Wild Dog), 15, 17, 25
Diabetes, 107
Dickens, Charles, 15, 42
Digging Behavior, 33
Dingo, 18, 25, 27
Doberman Pinscher, 66, 69, 72, 122, 126
Dog Association, 114
Dog Bowls, 101
Dog Health, 104
Dog Houses, 101
Dog Laws, 99
Dog Museum (New York), 49
Dog Shows, 114
Dog Stars, 58
Dog, History Of, 28
Doggerel, 40
Dogs In Art, 45
Dogs In Literature, 39
Dogs, Cruelty To, 36
Dogue De Bordeaux, 60, 122
Domestic Dog, 9, 14, 23
Draft Dogs, 64
Drinking, 78

E

Ears, Cropping, 77
Eating, 78
Egypt, 29, 33
Elderly Dog Care, 110
Epilepsy, 108
Europe, Medieval, 56
Europe, Renaissance, 35
Evolution, 11
External Parasites, 106

F

Feeding Dogs, 84
Fennec, 21
Fever Dogs, 54
Finnish Spitz, 122
Flat-Coated Retriever, 122
Florian, 41
Fox, 15, 19, 21, 25
Fox Terrier, 122
Foxhound, 122

G

Gazehound, 27
German Shepherd, 58, 70, 75, 81, 117, 123
German Shorthaired Pointer, 123
Giant Schnauzer, 128
Golden Retriever, 66, 69, 123
Gordon Setter, 124
Grapes, As Poison, 84
Great Dane, 60, 113, 123
Great Pyrenees, 123
Greater Swiss Mountain Dog, 123
Greece, 39
Greyhound, 17, 23, 29, 52, 61, 62, 124, 128, 129
Groenendael, 117
Grooming, 107
Guard Dog, 115, 118
Guide Dog, 36, 70

H

Haw, 79
Health Certificate, 100
Hearing, Sense Of, 21, 66, 70-71, 80-81, 111
Heatstroke, 108
Hip Dysplasia, 108
Homer, 39
Hot Spots, 108
Hound Of The Baskervilles, 56
Hounds, 34-36, 46, 61, 115
Humane Societies, 100
Hunting, 114

Husky, 64, 129

I

Ibizan Hound, 29, 124
Internal Parasites, 107
Iraq, 58, 67
Irish Red And White Setter, 124
Irish Setter, 124
Irish Water Spaniel, 124
Islam, Attitude Toward Dogs, 31
Italian Greyhound, 124

J

Jack Russell Terrier, 126
Jackals, 14, 15, 21
Japanese Chin, 124, 126

K

Keeshond, 58, 124, 126
Kennel Club (Britain), 115
Kerry Blue Terrier, 124
Kit Fox, 25
Komondor, 125, 127
Kuvasz, 125

L

Labrador Retriever, 66, 69, 123
La Fontaine, Jean, 40, 41
Lakeland Terrier, 125
Lamartine, Alphonse De, 41
Lassie, 43, 58, 60, 121
Lassie Come-Home, 43, 58, 60
Law Enforcement, 66
Lhasa Apso, 125
London, Jack, 43

M

Malamute, 23, 64, 116, 129
Maltese, 36, 125
Manchester Terrier, 126
Maned Wolf, 22, 25
Mastiff, 15, 29-30, 54, 113, 117, 122-123, 126-128
Mating Behavior, 89
Mesopotamia, 28
Mexican Hairless, 28, 130
Mexico, 28, 54, 58
Military Dogs, 67
Milne, A.A., 41
Miniature Pinscher, 126
Mixed Breed, 69

N

Neutering, 84, 98, 106
Newfoundland, 42, 64, 71, 122, 126
Norwegian Elkhound, 126

O

Old English Sheepdog, 60, 126
Old Yeller, 43, 60
Otterhound, 126

P

Pai Dogs, 32
Pancreatitis, 108
Panting, 78
Papillon, 46, 126
Parasites, 95, 106, 107
Pariah Dog, 27
Parson Russell Terrier, 126
Pasteur, Louis, 36
Paul Winter Consort, 80
Peat Dog, 26
Pekingese, 32, 75, 125, 127-128
Pembroke Welsh Corgi, 129
Persia (Ancient), 54
Petit Basset Griffon Vendeen, 127
Pharaoh Hound, 29, 127
Phu Quoc Dog, 18
Pit Bull, see American Staffordshire Terrier
Playing, 11, 58, 83, 87
Pointer, 36, 129
Poison, 84, 106
Polar Dog, 27
Police Dogs, 118
Polydactylism, 76
Pomeranian, 23, 42, 127
Poodle, 42, 55, 114, 124, 127
Portuguese Water Dog, 127
Psychic Dogs, 57
Pug, 114, 127
Puli, 76, 127
Puppies, 115
Puppy Development, 90
Pyrenean Mountain Dog, 69

R

Rabies, 30, 33, 36, 77, 99
Raccoon Dog, 19, 25
Red Fox, 25
Reproduction, 88
Retriever, 60, 70, 122, 123, 125
Rhodesian Ridgeback, 127
Rin Tin Tin, 58

Rome, 30, 39, 45
Rottweiler, 64, 66, 74, 127

S

Saint Hubert Hound, 34
Salem Witch Trials, 55
Saluki, 27, 29, 62, 128
Samoyed, 27, 116, 128
Schipperke, 128
Schnauzer, 118, 128
Scott, Sir Walter, 41
Scottish Terrier, 128
Search And Rescue, 69
Service Dog, 36
Setter, 124
Sheepdog, 64, 128
Shetland Sheepdog, 128
Shiba Inu, 128
Shih Tzu, 32, 77, 128
Show Dogs, 77
Siberian Husky, 129
Signal Dogs, 71
Skye Terrier, 129
Sled Dogs, 64, 115
Sleeve Dogs, 32
Smell, Sense Of, 21, 66, 69, 81, 87, 91, 94, 111
Smith, Owen, 61
Sniffing Behavior, 87
Socialization, 92, 98
Soft-Coated Wheaten Terrier, 129
Spaniel, 15, 42, 46, 119-121, 124, 129
Spaying, 98
Spitz Dogs, 36
St. Bernard, 40, 43, 60, 64, 69, 95, 113, 128
Staffordshire Bull Terrier, 129
Standard Schnauzer, 128
Submissive Behavior, 86
Sweat Glands, 78

T

Tail, 11-15, 17, 23, 29, 54, 72, 75, 77, 85-88, 92-94, 97, 110, 116-130
Tail Docking, 77
Tapetum Lucidum, 79
Taste, 78
Taxonomy, Science Of, 14
Teeth, 78
Teething, 94
Temperament, 114
Terhune, Albert Payson, 43, 56
Terrier, 19, 35, 60, 62, 114, 116, 117, 120-130
The Incredible Journey, 58
Thin Man, 60
Tibetan Spaniel, 129
Tibetan Terrier, 129

Ticks, 106
Toes And Claws, 76
Touch, Sense Of, 78
Train, 31, 67, 70-71, 82, 84, 92, 115, 117, 127, 129
Traveling With Dogs, 100
Treatment, 41, 45, 107, 111

U

United Kennel Club, 115

V

Vaccinations, 100, 105
Veterinarians, Choosing, 104
Veterinary Medicine, 36, 104
Vision, Sense Of, 79
Vizsla, 129

W

War, 9, 11, 15, 29, 31, 45, 67, 70, 93

Weimaraner, 49, 66, 129
Welsh Corgi, 64, 129
Werewolf, 9, 55
West Highland White Terrier, 129
Whippet, 27, 62, 113, 129
Whiskers, 78
Wild Dogs, 16
Wirehaired Pointing Griffon, 130
Wolf, 16, 22-26, 40
Wolfhound, 113, 117, 124
Worms, 107

X

Xoloitzcuintli, 28, 130

Y

Yorkshire Terrier, 114, 130

Made in the USA
Middletown, DE
18 October 2020